Praise f

M000104793

A MOTHER'S
greatest gift

"*A Mother's Greatest Gift* exactly identifies the greatest tool a mother has—access to personal revelation through the Spirit. If a mother can tap into that power, she has everything she needs to help parent her children. This book is rich with stories, examples, and guidance on how to access the Spirit and use the priesthood and other spiritual keys to help every mother. This book offers each of us the guidance we need to tap into the Spirit on behalf of our children. A tremendous help."

—Merrilee Boyack, author of *The Parenting Breakthrough*

"Heidi Poelman has discovered that the most important ingredient in the recipe for raising strong, successful, and happy children is each mother's ability to call on heaven through the Holy Ghost and through personal revelation to know God's will for our sometimes willful but often delightful children! Heidi teaches us that as we raise children in a scary world, our most valuable anchor can be sent down from above with power and love."

—Linda Eyre, coauthor of *Teaching Your Children Values* and
Five Spiritual Solutions for Everyday Parenting Challenges

"Heidi Poelman's book is a tremendous gift for mothers everywhere, a wonderful guide to seeking and relying on the Spirit as we raise our children. Drawing upon her own experiences and the experiences of other mothers, as well as the counsel and wisdom of the scriptures and Church leaders, Poelman has written a book that affirms, uplifts, and inspires the reader in ways that will bless her and her children. *A Mother's Greatest Gift* is a book I will return to again and again and share with every mother I know."

—Debra Sansing Woods, author of *Mothering with Spiritual
Power: Book of Mormon Inspirations for Raising a Righteous Family*

"With temptation only a click away, today's family is under attack like no other time in recorded history. Parents need all the help they can get to keep their family safe. Although every child is different and no parenting specialist can offer a promise for perfection, we do have a Heavenly Father who knows what's best in every situation. Heidi Poelman guides readers to this ultimate source for obtaining advice and acting on promptings received through the Spirit. I highly recommend this book to all parents."

—Randal A. Wright, PhD in family studies and author of
*The Book of Mormon Miracle, Power Parenting, Achieving
Your Life Mission,* and *Make Every Day Meaningful*

"*A Mother's Greatest Gift* is a fantastic read for any mother who is looking for words of inspiration and encouragement to bring the Spirit into her home and family life. Beautifully combining principles of the gospel with real-life motherhood experiences, this book feels like a comforting, powerful conversation with a friend who knows your life and wants to help you see the beauty in life when the gospel is at the heart of it. An absolute privilege to read!"

—April Perry, blogger at *Power of Moms*

"With stories of real women woven throughout, this book is a beautiful read for any woman who needs a gentle reminder that God is mindful of us every day. As mothers in a time when information is so accessible, it's easy to rely on ourselves without resting our hearts—our worries and insecurities—with the power who knows our families better than anyone else. For me, Heidi's book was a witness to God's love and concern for us as women, and it was a much-needed nudge to turn to Him more as I parent my children."

—Erica Layne, author of *Let Why Lead* blog

"*A Mother's Greatest Gift* provides wisdom, insight, and practical applications in seeking the Spirit for the challenging task of raising children. The shared personal experiences from the author and others are a valuable trove of support and inspiration."

—Linda Hoffman Kimball, author of *Apple Pies &
Promises: Motherhood in the Real World* and other books

A MOTHER'S
greatest gift

A MOTHER'S
greatest gift

*Relying on the Spirit
as You Raise
Your Children*

HEIDI POELMAN

CFI
An imprint of Cedar Fort, Inc.
Springville, Utah

ISBN 13: 978-1-4621-1605-8

Published by CFI, an imprint of Cedar Fort, Inc.
2373 W. 700 S., Springville, UT 84663
Distributed by Cedar Fort, Inc., www.cedarfort.com

LIBRARY OF CONGRESS CATALOGING-IN-PUBLICATION DATA

Poelman, Heidi N., 1980- author.
A mother's greatest gift / Heidi Poelman.
    pages cm
Includes bibliographical references.
ISBN 978-1-4621-1605-8 (alk. paper)
1. Motherhood--Religious aspects--Church of Jesus Christ of Latter-day Saints. I. Title.

BX8643.W66P64 2015
248.8'431--dc23

                        2014049019

Cover design by Shawnda T. Craig
Cover design © 2015 Lyle Mortimer
Edited and typeset by Jessica B. Ellingson

Printed in the United States of America

10 9 8 7 6 5 4 3 2 1

Printed on acid-free paper

For my *husband*, Scott,
for the *mothers* in my life,
and for my *children*

Contents

Contents

Acknowledgments

THIS BOOK is the product of the wisdom, testimonies, and experiences of several of my spiritual heroes. I would like to acknowledge the many authors who have researched and written about the topic of the Spirit, particularly Gerald Lund, whose extensive research and writings on the subject served to guide my understanding of how God communicates with us.

I would also like to thank the many people who helped shape this book. Thanks to my mother-in-law, Kerry, who first gave me the suggestion that our most important resource as mothers is our ability to listen for and act on promptings from the Spirit. Thanks to my mother, Susie, who raised me with unconditional love and taught me the beautiful promises of the gospel. Thanks to Scott, my husband, best friend, partner, sounding board, and the man who made me a mother in the first place. Also, thanks to all the incredible women who shared their stories with me and helped me see how willing Heavenly Father is to be involved in our lives. Lastly, thanks to my children for loving me while I learn and grow in this sacred journey of motherhood.

Introduction

I DON'T CLAIM to be a parenting expert. Like many parents out there, my primary desire is to give my children their best shot at happiness in this life and the life to come. This book is the result of a journey to discover more about what might just be the single best thing we can do for our children. It is the culmination of one mother's desire to better understand how to qualify for, receive, and act on personal revelation, which general Relief Society president Julie Beck has called the "most important skill that can be acquired in this life."[1]

My journey started with a comment from my mother-in-law, Kerry, a woman I admire deeply as both a person and a parent. Her five children are bright, well educated, service minded, well employed, fun loving, musically talented, and spiritually centered. I can't say I haven't been intimidated by that mothering legacy. From the moment I met her, I wanted to know more about how I could help my children follow in her children's footsteps and how I could follow in hers.

I asked her once, "So, what's your secret? Is there one parenting tip, one book, one resource you would suggest to help me figure out how to raise happy, successful kids?" I love parenting books and have devoured many in my search for the perfect parenting approach. I figured she had to have a favorite.

Introduction

Kerry didn't hesitate. "I think with every book I've read, I've picked out and applied different things that appeal to me," she said. "But what I'd say matters most is learning how to rely on the Spirit to guide you." It was so simple, and yet I felt the truth of her words immediately. Of all the books I could study, with all their different approaches and techniques, maybe it was the Spirit that could put all the pieces together to make a complete picture and answer every question I ever had.

It's often said that kids don't come with instruction manuals. And they don't. At least not in the way we typically think of instructions. As parents, what we do have is a communication channel that goes straight to an eternal God, a divine Parent, and to the One who knows each of our children better than does anyone on earth.

The messenger in that channel is the Holy Spirit, a member of the Godhead who connects each of us with our Eternal Father. The Spirit is our gift from the Father, which allows us to access our Creator at any time, as often as we want. As President James E. Faust once put it, "There is no limit on the number of times or how long we can pray each day. There is no quota of how many needs we wish to pray for in each prayer. We do not need to go through secretaries or make an appointment to reach the throne of grace."[2] What an awesome privilege. Our challenge is to grasp that privilege with both hands as we learn to communicate with our Heavenly Parent.

I thought about Kerry's suggestion. Surely, like many religious people, I had learned to pray. I prayed every day. I prayed about my children. I prayed about how I could be a good mother. But did I *listen*? Had I really learned to access that most important gift so that I could know the will of the Father regarding my children? Did I use that gift to provide comfort in times of trial? Was I teaching my own children to use the gift? I wanted to learn more.

I remember the first time it hit me, really hit me, how important my own role would be as a mother. I was pregnant with my first child, and I was on my way to the public relations firm where

I worked. Out of nowhere, the thought struck me, "I am going to have a son!" and I became emotional right there on the San Diego freeway. For whatever reason, in that moment, I felt an overwhelming realization that I was going to be given a precious spirit from my Father in Heaven. And He was going to trust me and my husband to care for that baby boy—to give him every-thing he would need to succeed physically, emotionally, mentally, socially, and spiritually. I imagine every mother has had a similar moment when she feels the significance of her calling.

I wrote this book especially for mothers—those who have borne their own children or are mothers at heart to the children in their lives. As mothers we hold the sacred stewardship of rais-ing and nurturing our children. No relationship in the world can compare to the unique connection and tender love between a mother and her child.

My journey to discover how the Spirit can guide and comfort mothers has been paved with several stepping-stones. Those stones include a study of what the scriptures and Church leaders have to say about personal revelation, my own parenting experiences with the Spirit, and interviews with mothers who shared with me how Heavenly Father has guided them. While some of the names of these mothers have been changed for privacy, all the testimonies shared here are true accounts of how mothers have been guided, warned, or comforted by the Spirit.

With every passage I read, and with every mother I inter-viewed, one conclusion became crystal clear: we are not alone while we raise our little ones. Our Father in Heaven wants to be with us all along the way. After all, our children are His children too. He wants to strengthen us, send answers to our questions, guide our decisions, warn us of danger, help us understand our children, and provide comfort when our hearts are aching.

I feel it important to note that although I refer in this book to our Heavenly Father as our Divine Parent and the One with whom we communicate, I believe that He works in partnership with Heavenly Mother, who is just as interested in our mortal success. We don't talk about her much, but we know that we are children of "heavenly parents."[3] We also know we can be exalted as celestial beings only as a husband and wife (see D&C 131). God, being one such exalted being, I imagine is subject to the same eternal rules. I love the lyrics penned by Eliza Snow, who wrote about our heavenly parents, "Truth is reason; truth eternal / Tells me I've a mother there."[4] From everything we know about godhood, about family, and about how God has asked husband and wife to be partners from the very beginning, starting with Adam and Eve, it seems clear to me that Heavenly Father works in partnership with His eternal companion. I believe Heavenly Mother is involved in our mortal journey, though we haven't been given the details on the exact role She plays. For the purposes of this book, I will keep to what we do know from scriptures and prophets about our communication with Heavenly Father.

The access we are granted to our eternal Father never wavers as long as we are worthy and willing to hear. From the time our little ones are born to the time they are grown, He is willing to play a role. As Kerry, whose children are all grown, shared with me, "Even today I felt inspired to connect with two of my older children. The one thing I will say for myself is that I know how to seek the Spirit. I know how to recognize it, and I know I'm nothing without it. I know it's Heavenly Father's plan to give us guidance all along the way."

What wise counsel to a young mother. That *is* His plan—to guide us all along the way. He has promised to always be there: "Draw near unto me and I will draw near unto you; seek me diligently and ye shall find me; ask, and ye shall receive; knock, and it shall be opened unto you" (D&C 88:63). He gives us that promise over and over throughout the scriptures. All He needs from us is a heart ready to receive His counsel and His comfort. If we are worthy of it, if we can learn to listen, and if we choose to act upon the spiritual promptings in our life, then our Divine Parent will show us how to best love our children and how to bring our families home.

Chapter 1

Motherhood

The Most Important Job on Earth
(and Why God Cares So Much)

I RECENTLY HEARD Sheri Dew at a conference telling a story about a young mother of three, eight months pregnant with her fourth, who was sitting at a fancy banquet with her husband. The mother was sitting next to the guest of honor, who at some point during the dinner leaned over and asked her, "So what do *you* do?" She felt reluctant to share, but she finally told him that she was a busy stay-at-home mom. The guest of honor simply said, "Oh," and turned to find someone else more interesting to talk to. This mother found herself feeling embarrassed that she didn't have something better to say for herself. For a moment, being a mother didn't feel like a grand and worthy occupation.[5]

I have been there. I have sat at those fancy banquets with my husband, with all the discussions of grand and important careers swirling around the table. I too have had moments of doubt when I looked back at all my years of education, at my prior success as a student, and at the distinguished careers of fellow classmates and have thought to myself, "What am I doing with my life? Why am I *just* home changing diapers and scrubbing bathrooms and mashing bananas? Why am I *just* a mother?"

Heidi Poelman

Our Divine Responsibility

The adversary is so terribly good at slipping those doubts into the minds of mothers for one very good reason: we are God's most powerful tools for accomplishing His most important work. He has told us so clearly about His number one priority: "For behold, this is my work and my glory—to bring to pass the immortality and eternal life of man" (Moses 1:39). That's what He wants *most*. He wants His children to return home and receive their own blessings of glory. How better to make that happen than to entrust His precious spirit children into the arms of a mother, who has the power to raise them in love and righteousness?

We are cocreators with our Father in Heaven and have a divine stewardship over His children. President Gordon B. Hinckley shared his perspective on how vital this partnership is: "Never forget that these little ones are the sons and daughters of God and that yours is a custodial relationship to them, that He was a parent before you were parents and that He has not relinquished His parental rights or interest in these little ones."[6] Indeed, our Heavenly Father is deeply invested in us. He trusts us, as mothers on earth, to help Him accomplish His mission for His children.

The job is so important that apostles of the Lord Jesus Christ have called mothers a type of savior of mankind. Elder Matthew Cowley of the Quorum of the Twelve stated that we as women "belong to the great sorority of saviorhood. . . . Men are different, men have to have something given to them [in mortality] to make them saviors of men, but not mothers, not women. You are born with an inherent right, an inherent authority, to be the saviors of human souls. You are the cocreators with God of his children."[7] President David O. McKay was also clear stating how he felt about mothers: "In her high duty and service to humanity, endowing with immortality eternal spirits, she is copartner with the Creator himself."[8] Elder Jeffrey R. Holland has shared similar thoughts about the sacred role, and sacred promises, of motherhood:

Mothers, cherish that role that is so uniquely yours and for which heaven itself sends angels to watch over you and your little ones. Yours is the work of salvation, and therefore you will be magnified, compensated, made more than you are. . . . The very fact that you have been given such a responsibility is everlasting evidence of the trust your Father in Heaven has in you.[9]

Can there be any doubt how our Father in Heaven feels about mothers? How can we ever say we are *just* mothers? I like Sheri Dew's suggestion for that young mother who was asked, "What do you do?" She said that mother might consider responding with, "I'm shepherding four children along the path to exaltation. How about you?"[10] If I am a mother, then I am blessed, trusted, and honored beyond measure in the eyes of God.

How Important Are Mothers?

One of my favorite accounts in the scriptures is the story of the armies of Helaman in the Book of Mormon. Consider it: Two thousand young men, probably just teenagers, willing to lay down their lives to follow a righteous leader and fight for the cause of freedom. They knew their God would deliver them. How did they know? Because of their *mothers*. We know that "they never had fought, yet they did not fear death; and they did think more upon the liberty of their fathers than they did upon their lives; yea, *they had been taught by their mothers*, that if they did not doubt, God would deliver them" (Alma 56:47; italics added). The tribute to their mothers was important enough to be inscribed in the sacred records of the prophets. They even "rehearsed unto [Helaman] the words of their mothers, saying: We do not doubt our mothers knew it" (Alma 56:48). The conviction in these young boys was so powerful that not a single soldier was lost, and the fate of a nation was altered forever. All because they knew their "mothers knew it."

Our modern-day prophets and leaders have promised that mothers today have the same power to influence generations to come. Elder Robert D. Hales said, "It is the spiritual preparation of our children in the rising generation that will, through their obedience, ensure the eternal preservation and perpetuation of our families for the coming generations."[11] President David O. McKay said that motherhood is "the noblest office or calling in the world." He explained the far-reaching impact of a mother:

> She who can paint a masterpiece or write a book that will influence millions deserves the admiration and the plaudits of mankind; but she who rears successfully a family of healthy, beautiful sons and daughters, whose influence will be felt through generations to come, whose immortal souls will exert an influence throughout the ages long after paintings shall have faded, and books and statues shall have decayed or shall have been destroyed, deserves the highest honor that man can give, and the choicest blessings of God.[12]

How much influence can a mother have? I dare say more than a chief executive officer at a big company or an architect with brilliant building designs, or even more than the man who first walked on the moon. Although noble and impressive in the eyes of the world, their impact is limited. A mother's influence is eternal.

When Kerry, my mother-in-law, was in sixth grade, her mother sat down on her bed and testified to her about the Book of Mormon. "The Spirit has told me that this book is true," she said. Kerry felt the Spirit too and started her own journey to know more. She gained a powerful testimony as she grew older and came to know and love the gospel. Now she has raised five children, who also live gospel-centered lives, and those children are teaching their children too. One woman can impact generations. How important are mothers to God's work and glory? They are perhaps the most vital key to the success of His plan. Mothers have the capacity to change everything. Luckily, God has not left those mothers alone to make it happen.

Chapter 2

The Holy Ghost

A Mother's Most Important Guide

LONG AGO, in a place we don't remember, we were part of a war in heaven. Two plans were presented. Each one of us who has come to earth made a choice to stand by our Brother, who offered His life for ours. We said we would go down to get a body, be tested, and prove our worth. Some of us would be given a sacred responsibility to teach others from the time of their birth. We would be charged with helping them understand everything they would need to do to return home to our loving Father in Heaven. We "shouted for joy" (Job 38:7) at the prospect and, I imagine, gave tearful embraces while we promised to do our best. One by one we were sent to earth. That's when we forgot everything.

Channel to Heaven

Of course, a loving Heavenly Father wouldn't leave us entirely to our own devices while we figure out this world. He sent along a lifeline, a communication channel, which we could use to reach Him any time. It wouldn't be easy, at least, not as easy as speaking to someone standing right in front of us. Indeed, that would be part of the test. Could we have the faith required? Would we seek Him? Would we listen closely enough to hear Him?

God communicates to His children through the Holy Ghost (or Holy Spirit). This is the means by which we receive personal revelation. The word *revelation* comes from the Latin word *revelatus*. The root *re* means "to draw back," and the word *velum* means "a covering or "veil."[13] So *revelation* literally means to draw back the veil. This is the gift God has given us here on earth: an ability to draw back the veil and hear the whisperings of heaven.

We Are Not Alone

How important is that gift as a mother? Several mothers shared with me how they simply could not do without the divine counsel of their Heavenly Father. My neighbor Pattie, mother of three grown daughters, put it this way: "Hacking your way through the 'what to do' jungle without some form of spiritual help or divine whisper inside, for me, seems impossible." I couldn't agree more. How much more overwhelming would it be to begin our mothering careers if we thought we were on our own to figure it all out? My friend Cary expressed to me her feelings about becoming a new mom and her prayerful realization:

> I recall not long after my first child was born. How I loved this precious child I had been entrusted with! The weight of responsibility I felt for her was a bit overwhelming. As a new parent I recall pondering many hours about how to teach my child how to distinguish right from wrong, truth from error. Our world can be so deceiving. In my prayers for an answer, I felt an impression and realized I had known all along what I needed to do. The Spirit was the key.

I love Cary's conclusion—the Spirit is the key to everything. We are not on our own. Our Heavenly Father has given us access to His counsel and comfort whenever we need it. One friend of mine needed it plenty while she raised her six children. Luckily, she knew just where to turn for help. As she said, "There have been times when I've felt overwhelmed with five boys. I remember praying and saying, 'This is so hard!' I received an answer that 'those are my children too. I will not leave you alone to raise them.' I realized I need to rely on Him more." In that moment, the veil was lifted just a bit so that this mother could experience a reminder of her previous home. She was given that simple reassurance that these are His children too. Those words came as personal revelation: *I will not leave you alone.*

Understanding how to draw back the veil and seek revelation from our Father in Heaven can allow us to receive the direction we need. We have a right to revelation from our Divine Parent. President Lorenzo Snow promised us this much:

> The Spirit of God . . . will reveal to [people], even in the simplest of matters, what they shall do, by making suggestions to them. We should try to learn the nature of this Spirit, that we may understand its suggestions, and then we will always be able to do right. This is the grand privilege of every Latter-day Saint. We know that it is our right to have the manifestations of the Spirit every day of our lives.[14]

In other words, if we can understand how to seek and listen for the Spirit, then we can receive counsel from our Divine Parent every day.

The Holy Ghost: Our Personal Guide

The purpose of personal revelation is for God to communicate with us by giving promptings, warnings, guidance, and comfort. Elder James E. Talmage described it as "the making known of divine truth by communication from the heavens."[15] Elder Gerald Lund of the First Quorum of the Seventy said that personal revelation is "communication of light and truth from the mind of God to the mind of man."[16] The way God communicates that light and truth is through the third member of the Godhead, the Holy Ghost.

Heidi Poelman

As Elder Lund explains, revelation is given "through the influence and power of the Holy Spirit. God is the *source* of all revelation. The Holy Ghost is the *medium* of communication."[17] Elder David A. Bednar put it simply: "Revelations from the Father and the Son are conveyed through the Holy Ghost."[18] The relationship between Heavenly Father and the Holy Ghost is also explained in the scriptures, where we read, "God shall give unto you knowledge by his Holy Spirit, yea, by the unspeakable gift of the Holy Ghost" (D&C 121:26), and by that Spirit "ye may know the truth of all things" (Moroni 10:5). This is Heavenly Father's gift to us: a way to communicate with Him through the Spirit, which can tell us all that we need to know and do, comfort us during times of trial, and warn us of dangers we cannot see. How does it work? By communicating in a way unlike anything else we're used to in this life.

My son Zach turned eight last year. He was baptized by his father, my husband, who afterward joined with a group of Melchizedek Priesthood holders to lay their hands upon Zach's head and ask him to "receive the Holy Ghost." That is the phrase used every time a person is given this gift.[19] Note the admonition to act. We are asked to "receive" the gift. This is not a passive experience. From the moment when Zach was given the gift of the Holy Ghost to be with him always, he was asked—he was expected—to *do* something. If we don't receive the gift by accessing it regularly, then the gift cannot bless us. As we are reminded in the Doctrine and Covenants, "For what doth it profit a man if a gift is bestowed upon him, and he receive not the gift? Behold, he rejoices not in that which is given unto him, neither rejoices in him who is the giver of the gift" (88:33).

In the days before and after the baptism, my husband and I were able to talk to Zach about what it means to have the Holy Ghost always with him and how exactly he might be able to utilize that gift. One important thing we asked him to remember is that God communicates with us in a way that is unlike any other communication we are used to in mortality. It is not like having a conversation with the person next to you, talking on the phone, or sending a text (wouldn't that be nice though?). The Holy Ghost communicates with our spirit.

As Elder Lund explains,

> [The Holy Ghost] does not communicate mouth to ear, or eye to eye, or hand to hand. He deals Spirit to spirit, intellect to intellect, feeling to feeling. He is not dependent on language. He needs no visas to cross country borders. He is able to impart light and knowledge completely individualized and tailored to the needs of the receiver regardless of age, culture, race, gender, intellectual capacity, or a host of other givens.[20]

His Spirit can communicate with our spirit anytime, anywhere, as often as we are ready to hear. Communicating that way takes practice and understanding, using our spiritual eyes and ears (see Matthew 13:15 and D&C 110:1). Here are a few rules to remember as we learn how to listen.

1. The Spirit whispers in a still, small voice. Typically, the Holy Ghost does not shout. (There are exceptions to this rule in the case of serious warnings, as I will discuss in chapter 6.) Most of the time, the Holy Ghost speaks in what we call a "still, small voice." This description can be found in the scriptures when the prophet Elijah describes the Holy Ghost after an earthquake. He writes, "And after the earthquake a fire; but the Lord was not in the fire: and after the fire a still small voice" (1 Kings 19:12). Joseph Smith described the voice similarly when he wrote in a letter to William W. Phelps, "Yea, thus saith the still small voice, which whispereth through and pierceth all things, and often times it maketh my bones to quake while it maketh manifest" (D&C 85:6). I find it interesting that although this voice is so small and gentle, it has the power to cause a prophet's "bones to quake."

The voice is "small" because it is not loud and obvious. But why is the voice "still?" Elder Gerald Lund explains it this way: "The voice of the Spirit is generally not audible. It does not create vibrations of sound in the air. It is a *silent* voice. It speaks to us through a different medium than sound waves. Thus, it is literally a still voice."[21] This is not a voice we hear in the same way we hear music, birds chirping, or the voice of the person next to us. Again, this is a voice we must hear with our spiritual ears.

Perhaps that is why the voice can be so easy to miss. If we are just listening with our mortal ears, if we are not tuned in spiritually, Heavenly Father cannot communicate with us. President Wilford Woodruff gave this warning: "Man is apt to look too high or expect too great things so that they often times mistake the Spirit of God and the inspiration of the Almighty. It is not in the thunder or whirlwind that we should look for the Spirit of God but in the still small voice."[22] If we want to hear, we need to be paying attention. If God has come knocking with a message and we did not notice, then "the Spirit will withdraw and wait until we come seeking and listening."[23] The still, small voice doesn't shout to get our attention. It will return when we are ready to listen.

2. The Spirit teaches line upon line. God reveals truth to us a little bit at a time. We are promised that if we take that little bit of truth and act on it, if we respond to it, then Heavenly Father will send us more. He is testing us, as the scriptures read: "For he will give unto the faithful line upon line, precept upon precept; and I will try you and prove you herewith" (D&C 98:12). In 2 Nephi we learn that God "will give unto the children of men line upon line, precept upon precept, here a little and there a little; and blessed are those who hearken unto my precepts, and lend an ear unto my counsel, for they shall learn wisdom; for unto him that receiveth I will give more" (2 Nephi 28:30).

President Henry B. Eyring explained it this way: "He sends truth line upon line, like the lines on the page of a book. Each time a line of truth comes to us, we get to choose what we will do about the light and truth God has sent to us. If we try hard to do what that truth requires of us, God will send more light and more truth. It will go on, line after line, as long as we choose to obey the truth."[24]

Isn't that a wonderful promise? We will continue to receive knowledge as long as we choose to receive it. But it won't come gift wrapped in a giant box all at once. As much as we may want the whole answer to our problem or the complete map that shows just how to move forward in life, the odds are that revelation won't come that way. Answers come one small bit, one line, one piece at a time. And why does Heavenly Father do that? Because "that pattern requires you to exercise faith."[25] God wants us to grow, and growth takes time and effort. If we want to see the finished puzzle, then we simply need to patiently take each piece He is willing to give, in whatever order and at whatever time He chooses to give it. If we can do that, then we will continue to get piece after piece, until we have the whole picture.

3. The Spirit comes as thoughts to our mind and feelings to our heart. The Spirit will not give one idea to our mind and a contradictory feeling to our heart. My husband, Scott, had an opportunity to learn this lesson personally fifteen years ago. At the time, we had been dating for a few months and had fallen quite in love. Then he went away to London for four months to do a study abroad for his English major. During that time, he started praying about marriage. He loved me, and we had become best friends, but doubts crept into his mind. The prospect of marriage was simply a scary one for a man whose parents had divorced when he was just a boy. Thinking he had his answer, Scott phoned me to break up. I, of course, was devastated.

A few weeks later and still traveling abroad, Scott attended a fireside given by one of my favorite BYU professors, Randy Bott. Brother Bott stood up to address the group and said that he had originally prepared a different message but had experienced a sudden prompting on the way over that he needed to change topics. The topic he felt prompted to discuss instead was the decision to get married and how the Holy Ghost confirms decisions. Scott was taken aback, to say the least.

During the fireside, Brother Bott read Doctrine and Covenants 8:2–3, which says, "Yea, behold, I will tell you *in your mind and in your heart*, by the Holy Ghost, which shall come upon you and which shall dwell in your heart. Now, behold, this is the spirit of revelation" (italics added). He explained that the Holy Ghost will not contradict Himself, causing one thought in your mind and a different feeling in your heart. The Holy Ghost will give the same answer to both. If your mind says one thing but your heart says another, Brother Bott explained, then most likely your mind is dealing with your own fear and not a personal revelation from God.

After the fireside, Scott went up to thank Brother Bott, expressing his belief that the prompting to switch topics was meant specifically for him. This BYU professor had no way of knowing that his chosen words that night would spark a change in the course of two young people's lives. That night Scott began to realize that although his mind had doubts stemming from fear, his heart said something different. It wasn't long before he was able to confront his fears, allowing his mind and heart to be in sync. He came back from London ready to move forward with the woman he hoped would become his wife (much to my relief).

Of course, thoughts and feelings from the Holy Ghost may come separately. A message from the Holy Ghost to the mind is like a thought coming out of nowhere that would prompt us toward something meaningful and good (as opposed to, say, a sudden pickle craving). As Elder Lund explained with a river analogy, "It is as though from time to time there is a soft plop as one of the Lord's 'pebbles' is dropped into this mighty Mississippi of our consciousness."[26] If that thought seemed to come out of nowhere, and if it is "in total alignment with the program of the Church,"[27] then it may be a whispering from the Spirit.

If a prompting does not come as a thought to your mind, then it will likely come as a sudden feeling or urge to do something. Being sensitive to the feelings of the Spirit is essential if we want to notice when God has something to say. As Nephi explained to his brothers, even seeing an angel did no good because "ye were *past feeling*, that ye could not *feel* his words" (1 Nephi 17:45; italics added).

Elder Dallin H. Oaks explained how he has experienced the Spirit regularly, not through an audible voice or clear thought but as a feeling: "Most of the revelation that comes to leaders and members of the Church comes by the still, small voice or by a feeling rather than by a vision or a voice that speaks specific words we can hear. I testify to the reality of that kind of revelation, which I have come to know as a familiar, even daily, experience to guide me in the work of the Lord."[28] Part of being open to receiving Heavenly Father's revelations is being ready to feel His influence.

4. The Holy Ghost is dependable. Scott's grandfather Elder Ronald E. Poelman was a member of the Quorum of the Seventy for several years. He once told us about an experience he had when he was first assigned to set up a new stake with President Gordon B. Hinckley, before he was called to be prophet. The two men traveled to the area where they were to set up a stake and call a new stake president. After meeting with several individuals, President Hinckley asked Elder Poelman whom he thought should be the new stake president. Elder Poelman, as the "greenie" elder, was surprised that President Hinckley asked him so readily for his opinion, especially since they had just met these men and knew hardly anything about them. After saying a fervent prayer together for guidance, President Hinckley, unruffled by Elder Poelman's concerns, gave him a pen and paper. He said, "Write down the name of the person who comes to your mind, and I'll do the same." So Elder Poelman nervously wrote down a name and showed President Hinckley. He smiled and showed Elder Poelman his paper. They had both written the same name. That experience was a testimony builder to Scott's grandfather that God is indeed involved in the details.

Elder Gerald Lund explains that this process of choosing new leaders is "one of the most challenging (and intimidating) things that General Authorities and Area Seventies are asked to do."[29] These visiting authorities are asked to do this in an area where they typically have no more than twelve hours to meet people and make a decision, and they sometimes don't even speak the same language! However challenging it may be, the authorities "look inward, reviewing feelings they have had or thoughts that have come to them," and then eventually they come to a consensus. "To an observer, the process would seem perfectly normal. But it works. Over and over, week in and week out in countries all across the globe. It works!"[30] I share Elder Lund's enthusiasm at how amazing this process is. God is there, and He is guiding His work every day, all over the world.

It is not just the leaders of the Church who have that constant and dependable guide. We too are promised that we may "always have his Spirit to be with [us]" (D&C 20:77). Not every once in a while, on a good day. *Always.* That is not to say we will receive answers and communications immediately upon asking, but we may always have His Spirit with us as long as we are worthy. Then, when the time is right, God will communicate with us.

I love the promise of President Spencer W. Kimball, who said, "Someone has said that we live in a day in which God, if there be a God, chooses to be silent, but [we proclaim] to the world that neither the Father nor the Son is silent. They are vocal and commune as proper and necessary, and *constantly* express a willingness, indeed an eagerness, to maintain communication with men."[31] From the mouth of a prophet—God is willing and eager to communicate.

How Do I Know It's the Spirit?

Separating our own thoughts and feelings from the gentle promptings of the Spirit is not always easy. I know I've been there, asking, "Was that just me?" or "Was that a message I should pay attention to?" I noted previously that occasionally a thought or sudden urge will seem to come out of nowhere. Elder Lund explains that if we act on that impression, often something will happen that confirms the message was from the Lord.[32] For example, President Wilford Woodruff shares an experience of when he was traveling with his family and they were all sleeping in their carriage for the night. He had a random thought enter his mind saying he needed to go move the carriage. It was not something he had been thinking about. He decided to act on that impression, not knowing the reason for it. When he told his wife he was going to move the carriage, she asked, "What for?" He responded, "I don't know." Thirty minutes after moving the carriage, a strong wind came and blew over a large oak tree, which fell right where his carriage had been. President Woodruff explained, "That was the still, small voice to me—no earthquake, no thunder, no lightening; but the still, small voice of the Spirit of God. It saved my life."[33]

Another thing to consider in deciding if a thought or feeling is from God is whether it inspires something good. If it feels right and inspires an action that is in line with the teachings of the gospel, then it very well may be a message from heaven. The Prophet Joseph Smith said, "They can tell the Spirit of the Lord from all other spirits. It will whisper peace and joy to their souls, and it will take malice, hatred, envying, strife, and all evil from their hearts; and their whole desire will be to do good, bring forth righteousness, and build up the kingdom of God. Tell the brethren if they will follow the Spirit of the Lord they will go right."[34] President Gordon B. Hinckley had a similar way of knowing whether a message was from God: "That's the test, when all is said and done. Does it persuade one to do good, to rise, to stand tall, to do the right thing, to be kind, to be generous? Then it is of the Spirit of God."[35]

About two years ago I had to ask that very question: Was this a message from heaven? Scott and I had three children, and that's what we had planned on having. I liked having three, and after growing up in a home with just me and one sister, three kids seemed like a nice little handful. As many mothers feel, I was often overwhelmed with the challenges of parenting three little ones, who were bright, busy, beautiful, and, at times, exhausting.

One day while we were at an extended family reunion, President Henry B. Eyring was addressing the group, telling a story about his brother. I had a sudden thought come into my mind about Zach (our oldest son) having a brother. Zach didn't have a brother. He had two sisters. As I drove home that day, that impression hung with me. I kept thinking about President Eyring and his brother, and I thought about how neat it would be for Zach to have a brother (not that you can even choose that!). Could that have been my own thought? Surely. But as Scott and I considered the idea over the next several months and started praying about it, we decided that it actually felt right to move forward and try for another baby. Indeed, Scott had been having his own feelings that there was a boy missing from our family.

I still don't know if that first impression was a message from God, but I believe it inspired me to do something that is in line with His plan. Now that our fourth little one has joined us, every person in our family is thrilled. And it turns out, that baby is a boy. Zach and his sisters finally have the brother I believe we were inspired to bring to our family.

One other guideline is important to remember when deciding if a message is from the Spirit: we will not receive revelation for someone else unless we have stewardship over that person. As Elder Gerald Lund explains, "We are entitled to receive inspiration in our lives and callings so we can live better and serve others. . . . However, unless we have a specific stewardship, that is, a priesthood or doctrinally based responsibility, over someone else, we do not receive revelation that seeks to *direct* or *correct* them."[36] We are not entitled to receive revelation for our neighbor or our mailman directing them to do something, although we may be inspired to act in some way that helps them. As mothers, we can know that we are entitled to receive inspiration for those over whom we have stewardship—our children.

Do we always know for sure if a message is from the Spirit? Maybe not. But we can find comfort in a promise from the scriptures: "Wherefore, every thing which inviteth and enticeth to do good, and to love God, and to serve him, is inspired of God" (Moroni 7:13). In other words, if it's good, then it's inspired. It's that simple.

What God Expects of Us

We know this: God is not going to whisper messages to us during every step of our mortal journey, and He will not whisper if we are not listening. He will only come to us if we are regularly seeking His influence. He will not impede our ability to struggle, to be tested, and to learn through faith. Just as an earthly parent cannot tell her child what to do with every decision, neither can our Father in Heaven. He expects us to use our own resources as we go along, and He expects us to come seeking Him in times of need.

When Oliver Cowdery wanted the opportunity to translate the Book of Mormon, he was unable to do so and wondered why. The Prophet Joseph Smith received a revelation explaining the problem. The Lord said, "Behold, you have not understood; you have supposed that I would give it unto you, when *you took no thought save it was to ask me.* But, behold, I say unto you, that *you must study it out* in your mind; then you must ask me if it be right, and if it is right I will cause that your bosom shall burn within you; therefore, you shall feel that it is right" (D&C 9:7–8; italics added). Oliver was not able to receive revelation because he did not use his own resources. He only asked and expected it to be given to him without more effort on his part. God expects more from us.

Elder Bruce R. McConkie reminds us of our responsibility:

> We're expected to use the gifts and talents and abilities, the sense and judgment and agency with which we are endowed. . . . Implicit in asking in faith is the precedent requirement that we do everything in our power to accomplish the goal that we seek. . . . We're expected to do everything in our power that we can, and then to seek an answer from the Lord, a confirming seal that we've reached the right conclusion.[37]

Once we have used our own resources, talents, and abilities, God expects us to seek Him early and often for guidance along our path. I love the picture of the Savior at the door with no handle. He is there, and ready, but we have to let Him in. The same thing goes for revelation from our Father in Heaven. He wants to communicate with us, but we have to reach out. We have to open the door.

President Spencer W. Kimball said, "The Lord will not force himself upon people, and if they do not believe, they will receive no revelation. If they are content to depend upon their own limited calculations and interpretations, then, of course, the Lord will leave them to their chosen fate."[38] Similarly, Elder Richard G. Scott reminded us that "the Lord will not force you to learn. You must exercise your agency to authorize the Spirit to teach you. As you make this a practice in your life, you will be more perceptive to the feelings that come with spiritual guidance."[39]

I love the yearning for spiritual guidance described in the Book of Mormon when the Twelve Disciples ask the Nephites to kneel and pray to their Heavenly Father. We read, "And they did pray for that which *they most desired*; and they desired that the Holy Ghost should be given unto them" (3 Nephi 19:9; italics added). Of all they could have prayed for, what they wanted *most* was guidance from their Heavenly Father through His Spirit.

Do we feel that passion for His influence? We know we must do everything we can to use our own gifts and resources in our life. At the same time, we must be seeking His influence, having a great desire to have the Holy Ghost to guide us. If we are doing that, and if we are living worthily, then Heavenly Father has promised to be with us.

Why It Is So Important

We have so many books in the world and so much information available to us on every device we own, from our televisions to our smartphones. Accessing knowledge seems easier than ever. We can choose to raise our children according to the world's resources and direction. Or we can choose to rely on a Heavenly Parent to guide us—a Parent with perfect knowledge who understands us and our children, through and through. If we choose to rely on Him, then we are given this promise: "If thou shalt ask, thou shalt receive revelation upon revelation, knowledge upon knowledge, that thou mayest know the mysteries and peaceable things— that which bringeth joy, that which bringeth life eternal" (D&C 42:61). We can know more than the information available to us in the world. We can utilize the perfect source of all knowledge and be directed in how to use that knowledge to bless our families.

Consider the words of Elder Richard G. Scott, who said, "In His plan of happiness, He included a provision for you to receive help with such challenges and decisions during your mortal life. That assistance will come to you through the Holy Ghost as spiritual guidance. It is a power, beyond your own capability, that a loving Heavenly Father wants you to use consistently for your success, peace, and happiness."[40] If we choose to receive His Spirit in our lives, then we will be able to know truth from error, we will receive warnings of danger, we will receive comfort in times of need, and we will be privileged to bring our families great joy as we learn and grow on our mortal journey.

Chapter 3

Promptings from Above

Guidance, Ideas, and Influence

IRECENTLY READ a story about a pregnant woman who went in to her doctor for a routine AFP test, a blood test that screens for birth defects. After the test, the doctor called to let this young mother-to-be know that the reading on the test had come back higher than he had seen in thirty years. Unfortunately, he explained, this test result meant the baby most likely had serious problems and would either not survive or would have major birth defects.

The woman was devastated and didn't know what to do. As she sat pondering, an idea came into her mind to pray for a miracle. She was surprised by the sudden prompting but thought she may as well try. That night she went home and followed the inspiration, praying for a miracle. On Monday morning she went in to the doctor's office to have the baby checked with the finest ultrasound available. The doctor expected the worst. But as he inspected the screen, he realized he could find nothing wrong with the baby. He told the woman, "Go home and testify that you have witnessed a miracle, for there is no mistake, no coincidence. This is nothing short of a miracle."[41] Where did that idea to pray for a miracle come from? Not from her. That idea came from her Heavenly Father, who knew exactly what she needed to do.

Because the success of Heavenly Father's plan has everything to do with the success of His children here on earth, He occasionally chooses to step in and give us direction on our path. He can't do that for every move, or we wouldn't experience the test of faith and endurance we need. But when He does choose to whisper some message that will bless and guide our path, He will do it through His Holy Spirit. Joseph Smith said, "A person may profit by noticing the first intimation of the spirit of revelation; for instance, when you feel pure intelligence flowing into you, it may give you sudden strokes of ideas."[42] Our Divine Parent is willing to give us ideas, guidance, and promptings to act in a way that will help our families succeed. In this chapter are stories from mothers who shared how God has done just that.

One way Heavenly Father sometimes guides us is when we need help with a sick or hurt child. My friend Stacey once received a prompting for how to help her baby boy, Greyson, who had the flu. Greyson's doctor told Stacey she needed to get him to drink fluids, but he wouldn't take anything. Worried about her son, she tried to think of what to do to help him. That's when she felt a prompting that made a difference. "I remember hearing a voice say specifically that I needed to buy some Gatorade and put it in a bottle," she said. "We had stopped giving him a bottle two months prior to this sickness, so I questioned whether it would work. But thankfully I followed that instruction. He was willing to drink down the fluid that way. By listening and following the Spirit, I was able to keep him from becoming dehydrated." Stacey heard a simple yet meaningful prompting, guiding her to act in a way that helped her son.

Heavenly Father also gives direction to help our children with their emotional needs. My friend Jenn is a mom to four cute young kids. She shared with me how spiritual promptings have helped her family: "There have been times when our kids have had busy schedules, or I was taking them from play date to play date, and the Spirit has prompted me to give them more home or just family time. Every time I have felt those promptings and followed them, I have been rewarded with happier children and closer sibling relationships." Again, when this mother chooses to listen for and follow promptings that come to her, her family is blessed. It doesn't have to be a huge, life-altering event for God to be involved. He sometimes chooses to whisper guidance even for the small things, like how to enjoy a peaceful night at home.

If we are listening closely, we may even hear the Spirit guiding us toward resources that are right at our fingertips. One mom shared with me her experience of having a sudden prompting to reach for a Church magazine that gave her an unexpected solution to a problem:

> Recently, one of my children was having a difficult time being kind to her sibling. While we were discussing this, I felt prompted to take a break from the actual discussion, which seemed to be elevating her frustration, and read the *Friend*. When we opened the *Friend*, it fell open to a story about how to be kind to your sibling. My child threw up her hands and said, 'Every time I'm having a problem, if I open up the *Friend*, it always tells me exactly what I'm supposed to do!' She obviously recognized the power contained in the *Friend* to help her. We talked about how Heavenly Father is aware of us and finds ways to speak to us if we are humble enough to listen. It also gave us the chance to talk about how much He loves us as individuals.

By dropping the simple idea of reaching for a magazine story, Heavenly Father communicated a message that helped one mother teach her child. I love the reminder that He is there to guide us along as we try to create love in our home.

Another mother attests that even family fun seems important to Him. One mother of six shared an experience of how a sudden prompting helped her create more joy and laughter in her home. "There was a time when one of my kids was struggling," she explained. "I felt we needed to laugh more. I had an idea to put different comics up on the fridge for the kids to see after school.

My kids would come home, look at the fridge, and laugh. That simple thing could guarantee an active, happy time after school. Who would think to do that? I don't remember how that came about. I just had a feeling that we needed to have more fun. Junior high can be the pits, but this made a difference. I think that was inspired."

Inspiration can sometimes fall right into our lap before we know we are going to need it. My friend Carla shared how an article she had read became just the tool she needed for her son later that same day. Carla explained that her teenage son had done something that had frustrated her. She asked him to go to his room, but she didn't want him just to sit there angry. She wanted him to think things over. As she walked out of her room, she suddenly thought of the article she had read earlier that day, which was a perfect fit for the situation. She brought the article to him and asked him to read it. "I knew I had been inspired," she said.

"I opened the door after a little while, and there was the sweetest, most beautiful feeling in the room," Carla said. "I knew the Spirit was there. There was a softening in him. I had been blessed earlier in the day with the tool I would need. My son thought that was a neat experience. He still remembers it. Our experiences prepare us. Tools are there for the taking. Something I just read or just listened to—God was dropping off a little tool."

Sometimes the guidance is simply in bringing to our remembrance something we already learned or read somewhere. Recently I had an experience when something I had previously read became a useful tool after a prompting jogged my memory. My son was having a hard time listening at the end of the day when we would ask him to get ready for bed, and he wanted to do other things. I was thinking over how I could best help him learn to be responsive and obedient when simply reminding him wasn't working well. I had a thought come into my mind of something I had read in a parenting book months previously. In the book, a mother had a son who wasn't a great listener. She decided to make little tickets that he had to earn by showing he was listening the first time she asked him to do something. If he earned enough tickets, then the boy could have his beloved teddy bear at night. It worked wonders for the mom in the book. I decided to give it a try.

We created some special listening sticks and let our son know he needed to earn five by the end of the day. He could earn a stick by doing the things he was supposed to do—little things like his job of loading the dishwasher, brushing his teeth, and getting his pajamas on—and responding quickly to his parents. We made a plan that if he earned five sticks, then he could have his favorite blanket at bedtime. That was just the motivation he needed, and though he's not perfect, our son got into a noticeably better habit of listening. It's such a small thing, having a memory come to mind that can help us with our children, but those little thoughts and ideas often come as guidance from a loving Heavenly Father.

Heavenly Father will also occasionally choose to guide us along when we are making decisions about how to handle a situation that can have a lasting impact on our children. My friend Carla shared how after her father died, her mother needed a lot of help around her house with things like cleaning and gardening. Carla knew she wanted her children to be involved, but she wasn't sure whether or not she should let her mother pay them for their work. While she was considering the situation, she had an idea come to her mind that she should not compensate them with money or gifts but rather let them feel the service.

"That choice became one of the greatest things we did for our kids," Carla said. "They weren't thinking of the gain, just the good feelings on the way. The joy of service is a completely different feel from the joy of earning money. When their grandma offered to pay them, they would say, 'No, Grandma, I really like the way I feel.'" Carla explained what a crossroads that decision was for their family, even though she didn't realize it then. Rather than getting paid for working, the family would work hard to help someone else, and then sit on the patio and enjoy the final result of their efforts with a greater form of payment than money.

Choosing early to focus on service made a difference in Carla's family. "Ever since that decision, my kids have always been willing to jump in and help," she said. "I'm forever glad that I chose to focus on service. Now my kids help their own kids to have that feeling of joy in their service. That will stand out in our family fabric." If Carla hadn't acted on the thought that came to her as she considered what to do, she may not have established this legacy of service in her family.

Heavenly Father may also use the Spirit to communicate messages to us about how to best help our children as they develop their talents and abilities. My friend Barbara said that once she was inspired with a thought for how to help her daughter, Leanne, prepare for a piano recital. The recital would be held at a grandmother's house. Leanne had been busy with track practice and only had one free night before the recital. Barbara said, "I was just cleaning house and a thought popped into my mind that this was the only night Leanne could go practice on Grandma's piano. The idea just flowed. So I texted her about the idea." Leanne responded, "Mom, that would be perfect." Leanne was able to go where she could practice for two hours and be prepared for her recital. "That was pure inspiration," Barbara said. "Neither of us were thinking about it, but it needed to happen. I started to tell Leanne about that process of inspiration, and now she's starting to recognize it too. The Lord truly does help us as mothers every day."

One mother, Shelly, was guided when she needed to find words of comfort for her daughter. Maya had applied to go to a girl's camp over the summer and had not been accepted. The sadness was multiplied when she found out her friend had been accepted. Shelly remembered sitting with her daughter. "I thought, *I don't know what to say.*"

Then seemingly out of nowhere, words came into her head, and she told her daughter, "Maybe there's a reason you couldn't go, and we just can't see it. We don't even know right now." Shelly didn't know why she said that at the time. Within a month, Maya's brother got his mission call. He would be leaving the same week

Maya would have been gone at camp if she had been accepted to the camp. Maya realized it and went to her mom, saying, "Mom, if I had gone to Quickwater, I would have missed the farewell!" As Shelly said looking back, "That was a little testimony to her that Heavenly Father is in charge. She found another camp that year, and she had no regrets. We just can't see sometimes."

We may not be able to see what's on the path ahead, but Heavenly Father can. He also knows what our children are going through even when we don't. That's why He will sometimes give us promptings to reach out to our children, and we may not understand why. As Kerry, my mother-in-law, described to me, "Sometimes I would receive little inclinations that I needed to stay up and be there when so-and-so comes home. Sometimes that's when they're the most teachable. Maybe it was the quiet of the night. When everyone else was asleep, that was a special time." Kerry has also had promptings to call her children when they have been living away somewhere. When that happens, she prays that she can say and be whatever her child needs at the moment. She explained how important that willingness to listen for promptings has been for her children:

> All of my kids have asked me, "How did you know I needed to talk to you?" I remember Josh asking me once, "Were you praying for me yesterday? I felt extra comfort." I had been. I told him, "Well, yeah, I was praying for you because I was worried." I don't think we realize how much our prayers can bless others, even if we never even talk about it. The more you listen, are humble, and are worthy of receiving the Spirit, the more it will come.

Kerry's whole life as a mother has been centered on that principle: if we listen and are humble, Heavenly Father will lead us along.

He also knows how to help us comfort our children in their times of need. Like the words that came into Shelly's head to comfort her disheartened daughter, sometimes we receive ideas that are not our own. My mom shared with me how she was prompted to help me when I went through my painful breakup with Scott. As she explained,

> You called me being so sad and sorrowful. I wondered how I could help you. I got the impression to share with you special scriptures that had helped me through the years when my burdens were very heavy and hard to bear. I wanted you to know that Heavenly Father and Jesus love you and know you, and that Jesus felt the very same pain that you were feeling, so He knew how to succor you. Just reading them again as I wrote down the references for you brought tears to my eyes. I knew that Heavenly Father wanted you to read those same scriptures, so that you might find peace and comfort.

That set of scriptures was a lifeline to me in a dark hour. I remember so clearly the large, white index card she gave me with dozens of scriptures written out for me to read. The activity itself of looking up each one gave me something productive to focus on. But more than that, the comfort I felt in all the reminders of love and hope I found in the scriptures brought me to a peaceful place. I never knew until I was working on this book that she felt inspired to do that for me. That alone is evidence to me that Heavenly Father is aware of me and aware of how He could help me through my mother.

Because Heavenly Father wants to help mothers as they raise their children, He will use the Spirit to prompt us and guide us to action. Whether it's a sudden prompting to make a phone call, a remembrance of something we had read earlier that would help our child in the moment, or an idea of how to comfort a child, He will communicate with us.

As President Ezra Taft Benson declared, "The Lord will increase our knowledge, wisdom, and capacity to obey when we obey His fundamental laws. This is what the Prophet Joseph Smith meant when he said we could have 'sudden strokes of ideas' which come into our minds as 'pure intelligence.' This is revelation. We must learn to rely on the Holy Ghost so we can use it to guide our lives and the lives of those for whom we have responsibility."[43] Our children are our greatest responsibility. Our Father in Heaven is ready to guide us with ideas that we didn't even know we needed, because He knows our children even better than we do. If we are listening for His voice, then we can hear His promptings, we can act upon them, and we can bless our families with everything He sees fit. Those promptings and answers begin with something as simple as a mother's prayer.

Chapter 4

Seek and Ye Shall Find

The Power of a Mother's Prayer

HEAVENLY FATHER has promised over and over again throughout the scriptures and through His prophets that if we seek Him, we shall find Him. One of the great privileges of having the Holy Ghost as a companion is that we can use that channel to our Father in Heaven when we are in need. He has said, "If thou shalt ask, thou shalt receive revelation upon revelation, knowledge upon knowledge, that thou mayest know the mysteries and peaceable things—that which bringeth joy, that which bringeth life eternal" (D&C 42:61). The answers we seek may not come right away, and they may not come in the way we expect, but they will come in just the way He knows we need them most. As mothers, if we will ask, if we will seek, then we can know through the Spirit what we need to know to bring our children joy.

I have found Heavenly Father's answers even in what seems like fairly routine parenting moments. One night, I was having a hard time with my three young kids at bedtime. Two of them were fighting over something, and no one was listening. I kept asking them to go get their pajamas on and brush their teeth. My oldest looked at me and said, "I don't like it when you tell me what to do." I felt heartbroken and beaten down by the time everyone was finally tucked into bed. I certainly wasn't feeling like a very good mother.

I walked into my room and turned on some bath water, hoping a good soak would soothe my frustrations. I knelt down and prayed that I would know how to help my kids be kind and respectful to each other and to me. After that, instead of grabbing the new novel I was considering as a distraction, I felt a sudden desire to pick up a parenting book by Linda and Richard Eyre that I had started reading several months before. I flipped it open to where I had left my bookmark. The subject of that chapter was remembering that our children are our spirit brothers and sisters with their own agency and divine heritage. The book suggested that keeping that in mind would help to create an environment of respect. I had to smile at what had to be more than coincidence. That chapter, falling in my lap right when I was seeking guidance, was an answer to my prayer. I'm not going to say that chapter was the magic bullet that made everything perfect in my house from that day forward. But the perspective change for me made a difference as I tried to move forward with a tone of mutual respect in our home. It also reminded me that we are not alone as we parent our children—Heavenly Father is aware of our needs.

A similar drop of guidance came in a different difficult hour when I was on my knees asking for advice. I was having another one of those nights when things weren't running as smoothly as I wanted, and I was simply feeling the burdens of motherhood. (Perhaps I should note that I tend to be a bit of a perfectionist, so my tolerance for chaos and sibling squabbles is not as high as I would like. I think Heavenly Father knows this about me.) After I ended my prayer, my eyes went straight to a sign I have sitting by our bed—a sign that has been there for ages, so I hardly notice it now. But after this prayer, the words jumped out at me: "Count Your Blessings." I smiled and felt the distinct impression that this was a message from my Heavenly Father, who knew I needed a simple perspective change. Sure, being a mom is hard.

But I had so many things going well, so many blessings. That's what I needed to focus on.

Another time, I received an unexpected answer after asking for help to know how to comfort a child who had her feelings hurt at school. This wasn't a life-or-death situation, but no mother wants to see her child suffer, even for a moment. My little kindergartner, Ellie, had come home one day upset about a friend. She told me that her friend had run away from her at recess, causing Ellie to feel left out. Earlier that week, Zach had had a similar experience when a friend told him he didn't want to be in his field trip group. Both of these experiences had broken my heart. Usually my kids are confident and happy with their friendships, and I haven't had many opportunities to worry about them feeling included. But that particular week, my heart ached for my little ones who had been hurt. I prayed to know how I could help them and how I could teach them. Again, it was a simple plea from a mother who wanted her children to feel loved wherever they go.

Just a few days later, I was in Ellie's class for a science project and saw her sitting on the rug giggling with that same friend who had hurt her feelings at recess. I looked around and noticed two other girls who seemed to each be sitting by themselves. I had a strong impression that I needed to teach my children something about friendship. Rather than worrying over who would or wouldn't be their friend that day in the fickle world we live in, I needed to teach them to look for others who needed a friend. It was a thought that seemed to come out of nowhere. As I considered the thought, I knew that Heavenly Father had answered my question of how to help my children in the realm of friendship. I went home and shared my feelings with them. I let them know that the best thing we can do in our times of sadness is to look outside ourselves and bring happiness to someone else. That's a lesson I hope to remind them of over and over as they make their way in the world.

A friend of mine, Melissa, had a similar experience receiving answers to her parenting pleas. One recent answer surprised her.

But after she acted on it, she knew she had been guided to a parenting approach that worked for her child:

> One of my children is harder to parent than the others. I feel like we had tried every method of discipline we knew of. Nothing was working. I prayed to know what I could do to help this child. An idea came to mind to hold this child and love this child and make this child hold and love me until he was calmed. I thought it was just a crazy idea I had imagined up. I prayed some more and had the same thought, so I decided to try it. Guess what? It worked. It wasn't a crazy idea I had cooked up. It seems that this child doesn't know how to de-escalate himself very well, and getting him to do this helps him relax and listen to me. I am then able to discipline gently, and this child responds better to me now. I credit that to the prompting I had.

Melissa had prayed for help, and she had an idea come to her that worked for her child. That's another testament to me that God knows our children even better than we do.

While some prayers are answered suddenly in surprising ways, other answers come slowly. Usually that's for a reason. My friend Laura had an experience with bringing children to her family when answers to prayer were a long time coming. Only later did she understand why. After having her first child, Laura had a hard time getting pregnant again. She had to have a procedure done, which doctors promised was successful 95 percent of the time. After four years of trying, Laura still wasn't pregnant.

"I was starting to question why we weren't receiving the blessings of more children," Laura said. "I felt like Alan and I were good people. We felt like we were good parents to Colton." Their oldest started asking when he would have a brother or a sister, and Laura was wondering too. Tired of the complications, the shots, and the emotional turmoil, Laura and her husband started thinking about adoption. "I was having a conversation with Heavenly Father," Laura explained, "and I said, 'I'm ready to stop all these shots. I want to adopt.' A wonderful peace came over me, and I knew it was the thing to do. Alan came home that night and as we talked, he felt the same way. We started the process right away, and about nine months later we had a little girl." They named her Sarah. Grateful to have a boy and a girl in their family, Laura thought that was it. Then, a little over a year later, she learned something that surprised her—she was pregnant. The answer to her prayer for another baby just needed a little time so God could give an extra blessing to this family.

"I have felt so strongly that Sarah was meant to be in our family," Laura said. "Several people have asked if Sarah and Carter are twins. So often I forget she is adopted! My grandfather, father, and I were fast runners in our youth. Sarah is also fast, and I would tell her she gets it from my side of the family. She is ours!"

Four years of feeling like prayers were going unanswered, and yet it was all for a reason. Heavenly Father wanted to bless this mother with children, but He knew a little girl was meant to be in their family. If He had blessed them with the second pregnancy they had prayed for right away, Laura and her husband likely would never have adopted. And so He waited. Once Sarah was where she belonged, more blessings followed.

Sometimes answers come in disguise. One mother told me about a time when her daughter was making poor choices. She had moved in with an older man who was not religious and who had an eleven-year-old daughter. The mother prayed for inspiration about what to do. The family continued to show their love and support and invited her home for Sunday dinners, where everyone could laugh and enjoy their time together. Beyond that, they weren't sure how to help their beloved daughter.

Then this mother and father were called to be the liaison couple to a young adult ward, often attending the ward's activities. At that point, their daughter was acting as a mother to this eleven-year-old girl and had slowly started realizing that her life as a young adult wasn't what she wanted. "She would come for dinner, and we would tell her about the fun activities the kids were doing and how many great guys and gals were there," the mother explained. "Our daughter realized that her life wasn't so fun and carefree. She eventually asked if she could move back home and attend church with us at the young adult ward. We introduced her to the great people there, and she was really embraced by them. She came back to church and back to being active." What first seemed like a typical ward calling was actually an unexpected answer to one mother's prayers. "That was truly a blessing," she said. Without that calling into the young adult ward, this mother and father may never have been able to share the stories with their daughter that motivated her to change course.

Heavenly Father also occasionally opens a door to a new place when we are feeling stuck. One mother, Sherry, shared with me how a sudden opportunity to exit a negative situation was just the answer she needed to help her daughter. Amy had fallen in with a group of friends that was having a negative influence. Despite Sherry's best efforts to persuade or discipline, nothing was working. "After a lot of trying to find an answer as to how to handle the problem, and the intensity of lies and screaming at home, we realized we needed help," she said. "The other children needed to not have this as a daily battlefront." Sherry prayed for a way to help her daughter, knowing that she needed distance from this group of friends in a safe place, but also not wanting Amy to feel they didn't love her or were embarrassed by her choices.

As these concerned parents considered options, a phone call came from Amy's grandmother, who had just moved away. Sherry's husband started talking to his mother about the situation. The grandmother had an idea. Someone in her ward was looking for temporary help setting up a new office. As Sherry explained, "Grandma called and asked Amy to come live with her for the summer. She let Amy know that her friend had a temporary job and wondered if she would like to do it. After reflecting on it more, we felt that her calling may have been the answer to the prayer we had been searching for."

Amy decided to take her grandmother up on the offer and move away from home for a few months. The decision made a significant difference in her life. As Sherry put it, "It still took time for her to find her path, but I do think it was an answer that truly helped. She has become the most amazing, patient mother with her two sons and has grown into an extraordinary person."

It was only after Amy left to move in with her grandmother that Sherry found out more of how the Spirit was guiding multiple people to find a solution. The grandmother had just found out that the man in her ward needed help setting up the office for a few months. Then her son told her about the situation with his daughter. Puzzle pieces were falling into place. As Sherry explained, "After some time, my mother-in-law shared that she had the oddest prompting to call us. It was perhaps two mothers' and a father's answer to the best direction for our daughter. I have always felt our Father in Heaven was setting up the opening at the office, the new place my mother-in-law just happened to find to live, and the call she just happened to make." Looking back on the experience, Sherry is confident that Heavenly Father was aware of this little family and that the Spirit was able to guide and bless them as a result of their pleas for help.

Another example of when the Spirit helped guide a mother on a new path occurred in my own family. When I was young, my parents decided to divorce, and my mother needed to find a new home for herself and her two daughters. She had two weeks to find the right place. Based on her income, she says, "What we really could afford would have been a condo, an apartment, or something in a rougher part of town. But that isn't where we ended up." She told me, "I prayed that I would find the right house for us. And when I saw our little house, the Spirit whispered strongly to me that this is where I was supposed to raise my girls."

Though she knew it would be tight, she was able to make the payments working night shifts as a nurse. I was able to grow up in a beautiful neighborhood with good schools and good, strong families. "I think both you and your sister might not have had the opportunities you had, especially with education, if we had not stayed there," she said. I am so grateful that my mother recognized and followed the Spirit as she decided where to raise her children.

In addition to guiding mothers with whisperings in their minds or feelings in their hearts, the Spirit often guides us with answers in the scriptures and from prophets. As Elder Dallin H. Oaks has said, "The best way to have the spirit of revelation is to listen to and study words spoken under the influence of the Holy Ghost. In other words, we obtain the Spirit by reading the scriptures or reading or listening to the talks of inspired leaders."[44] We have so much spiritual direction right at the tips of our fingers, ready for the taking. When we want to find answers, after we have prayed, we can go to the scriptures and to general conference addresses and seek inspired messages.

My friend Julie shared a scripture with me that has been helpful as she has faced parenting dilemmas. Alma 31:5 says, "And now, as the preaching of the word had a great tendency to lead the people to do that which was just—yea, it had had more powerful effect upon the minds of the people than the sword, or anything else, which had happened unto them—therefore Alma thought it was expedient that they should try the virtue of *the word of God*" (italics added). The word of God has a powerful effect.

Julie had been struggling one night, trying to know what to do about a specific child's behavior. She prayed for help and then got on LDS.org, "looking for something . . . anything," she said. Within five minutes of her search, she came across a quote by Elder Boyd K. Packer, who said, "The study of the doctrines of the gospel will improve behavior quicker than talking about behavior will improve behavior."[45] She realized that the scriptures were the answer, as she explained:

The word of God is more powerful than the sword. Preaching the word changes people's very nature. All of those books I had been reading on parenting went out the door. I realized through this divine revelation what we needed to do was read the scriptures more consistently and more in depth. We studied scriptures on behavior, but also stories about Nephi and Abinadi and Ammon. I think the mere act of coming together to obey God's word and to study has completely changed the spirit in our home as well as our children's behavior throughout the day. I can't explain how this works in scientific terms, but if we obey, God will do the rest!

This isn't to say we should ignore parenting books. I have many that I love and refer to regularly for the treasures of knowledge outlined by experts. Julie simply had an experience realizing that the scriptures needed to be her first go-to source. More gems of wisdom are available in the scriptures than in any other book we could possibly read. Heavenly Father will send answers as we seek. Then we can prayerfully supplement with other sources as we see fit.

My friend Abby similarly realized how precious the scriptures are as a parenting resource when she was trying to learn what to do about a child who was challenging for her. She checked out a stack of parenting books from the library and placed them on the nightstand next to her scriptures. She started going through the library books in search of an answer, but she wound up feeling unsatisfied.

"The books I read were conflicting, time consuming, and seemed to lack something," Abby said. "After a lot of prayers, I soon realized the best parenting book was one I had had for a lifetime. I returned the parenting books and turned to the scriptures. When I study the scriptures as a parenting book and seek for the Spirit to guide me instead of a book written by someone that has never met my children, behavior seems to be a little more manageable."

Again, this isn't to say that other sources of information are useless. Many wonderful books offer valuable insights that can help us along in our parenting. But for this mother, the answers she needed were first and foremost in books of scripture penned by inspired prophets of God. Our Father in Heaven is always there to guide us as we study, if we study prayerfully. He can help us assemble the pieces. He will lead us through His Spirit to the

Heidi Poelman

answers we seek, and those answers will be tailored to our own individual situation because He knows us.

We may not find answers to our prayers exactly when we ask for them and in just the way we expect. We may not even realize we have been given answers until we look back upon our experiences. He might choose to answer through a prompting in our thoughts, a feeling in our hearts, a phone call from an inspired relative or friend, a sudden opportunity, a conference address from an inspired leader, or a verse in the scriptures. What we can count on is this: Heavenly Father is aware of us, He hears our prayers, and He will send answers in whatever way and time is best as long as we are open to receiving them.

Chapter 5

When God Takes the Reins

Stories of Divine Intervention

B ABY CHASE was born fifteen weeks early. He was tiny and fragile, weighing in at two pounds, one ounce. His mother, Stephanie, was constantly prayerful that Chase would be strong enough to make it. After three months, little Chase was still in the hospital. Among other things the doctors were watching, Chase's retinas were being pulled back by abnormal blood vessels, a condition known as retinopathy of prematurity that can lead to blindness. Chase had an appointment to be seen by a specialist from another hospital the next week. That specialist happened to be visiting Chase's hospital and was in the room checking on the intensive-care babies. A nurse decided to point out Chase to the doctor. "That's the baby you'll be seeing next week," she said. The doctor looked over at Chase and responded, "Why not now?"

The doctor examined little Chase a week ahead of schedule and realized that he needed immediate help. As Chase's grandmother Carla explained, "We learned that if the baby had waited a week to be seen, the blood vessels would have pulled the retinas out of place, and he would have gone blind." This boy is now a bright and capable nine-year-old whose eyes are just fine. If that nurse hadn't had the thought to point Chase out to the doctor, and if that doctor hadn't felt like he should examine the baby that day, then life would have been dramatically different for Chase. Heavenly Father knew this baby was going to make out okay. He just needed to intervene a bit.

Perhaps we are quick to think that surely God wouldn't intervene in matters where just one tiny baby is being affected. God would only step in to adjust the course for events that would have some major impact on humankind. Consider what Elder Gerald Lund has to say on the matter: divine intervention happens "when, in a very natural way, things fall into place so as to provide us an answer we seek or a solution we need or to take us in a direction we need to go." He says, "These happen more commonly than some might think."[46] If Heavenly Father knows that a particular course needs to be taken in a person's life, He will intervene, whether that is for health and well-being, safety, or an important decision that will impact that person's future. His willingness to occasionally take the reins is one more way we can know of His great interest in our lives and His desire for us to succeed.

One way our Father in Heaven may intervene is by planting an idea in our minds that can change the course of events. One grandmother shared with me a story about her grandson, who at age three still refused to talk. The more people tried to get him to speak, the less he would. The grandmother said to me, "I felt impressed that my husband and I needed one-on-one time with him. There was so much going on in his family, and he was left out a bit. I talked to his mom, and she had been thinking the same thing." So the grandmother picked him up every day in the afternoon and the boy would play at his grandparents' house for a few hours until his mom came to get him. They did that for a month. Then one day when all the family was gathered, this little boy ran up the stairs, calling, "Nana, Nana, Nana!" Silence followed. "Everyone was stunned," his grandmother said. "That was a breakthrough. After that, he gradually started talking. The one-on-one time changed everything."

What seemed like a fairly simple idea actually had a big impact on this family, and the grandmother who shared her story feels without a doubt that the idea didn't come from her. Heavenly Father had helped steer the family in the right direction to help their little boy.

Heavenly Father is also interested in the health and well-being of His children and will sometimes intervene when a prayerful mother needs help. My friend Abby shared a story about when her son Oliver had been sick for six months. "Our doctor diagnosed him with something I knew was incorrect," she said. "I felt prompted not to follow the doctor's orders and treatment." Abby wanted to make an appointment with a specialist but knew that she would not be able to get Oliver in for a few months because the doctor's schedule was full. But perhaps Heavenly Father knew this appointment was too important to wait. As Abby explained,

> During a very busy day, I was prompted to call the office and ask a few questions. While I was on the phone, someone called and canceled an appointment scheduled for that afternoon. We were able to drop everything and make it to this specialist, who was booked two and a half months out. After a lot of testing, Oliver was diagnosed with a serious infection that would possibly have caused lifelong complications had it not been caught immediately.

Abby said that if she had followed the first doctor's prescribed course, Oliver could have been seriously hurt due to the nature of his infection. Thankfully, Abby listened when the Spirit guided her against that course of action. She continued to follow the promptings she received as she called the specialist at just the right time, when an appointment was made available. Coincidence? Maybe. But as the popular saying goes, "There are only two ways to live your life. One is as though nothing is a miracle. The other is as though everything is a miracle." To this young and in-tune mother, the path that led to answers for her son was plain evidence that Heavenly Father was aware of their situation and was guiding her course.

Another mother had a similar experience of feeling guided to help her daughter. Karen's daughter had suffered for years with an eating disorder. After many visits to a psychiatrist and years of struggling through high school and college, the daughter finally decided that she wanted to go to a center where they had in-patient counseling. Karen was considering whether she and her husband should send their daughter to the counseling program when she happened to tune in to a radio program that impacted her course.

The story on the radio was about the importance of family members giving money to help each other. "I realized that we needed to support our daughter so she could attend this program," Karen said. "Then I went to the temple and received a strong witness that she needed to go. We sent her, and it changed her life. She was able to get over her addiction. That was the result of two powerful promptings." It is this mother's testimony that Heavenly Father knew what would help her daughter through her trials. He just needed to drop a hint at just the right time that would guide them along in the right direction.

The Spirit will sometimes literally tell us to change direction if we are going the wrong way. That's what happened when my sister Shannon was in elementary school, in a time before cell phones were a regular convenience. My mother needed to leave the house to run some errands after she had sent us girls off to school. As my mother explained, "When I had gone about three blocks away, the Spirit whispered to me that I needed to go back home." What an unusual prompting for a mother on a typical outing. But she couldn't shake the feeling that she needed to turn around. So she stopped the car, turned around, and drove back home. "As soon as I got home," she said, "the school called to tell me Shannon was sick and needed to be picked up." No cell phone? No problem. Heavenly Father has His ways of communicating with us. Luckily for Shannon, my mother was willing to hear His call.

Sometimes Heavenly Father helps direct our course through someone else. As Elder Richard G. Scott has said, "On occasion the Lord will give us vital spiritual guidance by inspiring others to share what they have learned. Such mentors can greatly enrich our lives through thoughtful communication of their knowledge and experience."[47] Indeed, sometimes these mentors come just when we need them most and, without even knowing it, make a life-altering impact.

Leslie is a mother who had an unexpected run-in with one such mentor. Leslie had been taking her son to doctors and psychologists for months, trying to understand her teenage son's condition. She knew something was off, but none of the doctors she visited were able to help. She finally came to the realization that Heavenly Father knew her son better than any physician ever would. "A lot of times, I thought I could solve it myself," she said. "Finally, after I had tried everything I could think of, I knew it wasn't enough. I was finally willing to pray."

Leslie started praying to be led to the right people who could help her know how she could help her son. Shortly after she started asking God for direction, she ran into an old friend at the grocery store. Seemingly out of the blue, this friend started to tell Leslie about her two sons who had a condition with symptoms just like Leslie's son. Leslie had known this woman for years, but this topic had never come up before. As Leslie listened closely to her friend, she realized this was the guidance she had been waiting for. Hopeful, she asked for more information.

Leslie took her son in to see the doctor her friend had recommended. After reviewing the case, the doctor told Leslie she had already nailed the correct diagnosis. Relieved, this mother knew she was finally on the path to solving a mystery that had puzzled her for so long. Now with the right doctors and treatment plan, she was able to start getting her son the help he needed. "I went back to the other doctors, and they couldn't believe how blind they had been," Leslie said. "This was just a chance meeting with an old friend at the store. Why did we even stay and talk? That was a real turning point. Until that happened, we were blind. So blind. My friend was there the day I needed her." Surely that meeting didn't happen by chance. This was a drop of divine guidance given to a prayerful mother through an inspired friend.

Heavenly Father may also choose to prompt us to change our course when He knows the new direction will be for our greater happiness. My neighbor Pattie had been able to get through two difficult pregnancies and have healthy babies. But then she suffered a miscarriage with their attempt for a third child. She was grateful for her two children and came to the conclusion that she and her husband would not have any more. Heavenly Father had other plans for this family.

"My husband was the person who received the prompting that there was a very strong spirit that needed to be brought to our family," Pattie said. "For some reason, this spirit was to be raised by us." Pattie was skeptical after hearing her husband's proposal and tried to push back, saying that getting pregnant again wasn't a high-level priority for her. "With all that was going on in my life at that time, I had to do a lot of praying and acceptance," she said. "I had to find the faith that my husband actually heard this message correctly."

Pattie finally came to the conclusion that there was indeed another child waiting to come to their family. She was able to get pregnant and had another daughter, who is now grown. "To tell the rest of the story," she said, "this daughter has the most wonderful insight and manner about her and is highly regarded in her field. She is a great blessing, and that strong spirit is definitely one of her traits." Heavenly Father knew this daughter needed to be in Pattie's family, even if Pattie had originally decided on a different course of action. Luckily, Pattie was willing to be open to her husband's prompting.

Heavenly Father also occasionally intervenes to stop us right in our tracks if we are heading down a road that may cause us harm. My friend Carla was getting ready to leave for the day when she had a strong feeling that she needed to stop and say a prayer. "I just stood in the archway of the door and prayed," she said. Then as she was leaving in her car to run errands, she had the feeling that she needed to take a different route than normal. So she drove a different way. "I also had a feeling that I should take a phone call from my daughter-in-law," Carla said. "I didn't really have the time, but I sat in the car and visited with her." That's when Carla saw two fire trucks coming down the road.

"I went to a church parking lot on a hill to look down on the road to see what had happened," she said. "There had been a massive car accident with multiple cars. A girl had swerved into oncoming traffic. If I had not changed my mind and decided to go another way that day, there's a huge chance I would have been in that wreck. You never know if a delay that day could have saved your life." Carla will never know for sure what would have happened if she had ignored her prompting to pray, ignored her prompting to take a different route, or ignored her prompting to take that phone call. But she feels strongly that those promptings were all gentle nudges from her Heavenly Father, who wanted to keep her safe.

Another mother, Linda, told me she feels like Heavenly Father may have been involved in keeping her son safe by prompting him to skip a trip outside the country. Sam had planned to be in Brazil for the summer to study. He had been told by a roommate from Brazil that he would be fine as long as he wasn't going to Rio, which he was. Sam figured he would be fine since he would just be going to school. The roommate said he'd be fine as long as he wasn't going to be downtown a lot. Then Sam found out that he would have to walk downtown a mile to school every day. Linda started feeling unsettled about the trip. "So many things were not coming together," she said. "I started praying that he would real-ize it was not a good idea."

One problem, besides the location, was that the company sponsoring the trip had not been in touch with Sam at all about preparations. According to Linda, six or seven things were not in place that should have been. The day before he was supposed to leave the country, the company finally sent an email about the books he would need to bring. But it was too late to get the books in the States, and shipping them to Brazil would cost too much. That was the last straw. "Finally he entertained the idea of not going," Linda said. "I thought, *Thank you, thank you for not sending that email earlier.* I just felt like he shouldn't be going. Now he's in Africa, and I feel much more calm. I think the Lord just hit me over the head. I don't know if anything would have happened to him in Brazil, but I'm glad he didn't go."

Of course, no one can prove whether God was actually involved in influencing these events. That's not something we can test the way a scientist would test a hypothesis. Maybe chance played a role. Maybe it was just coincidence. Maybe it was what some would call "mother's instinct." Maybe. What I know is this:

1. God cares what happens to His children.
2. He is willing to play a role in our lives.
3. He is able to communicate with us and give us messages that will bless our lives.
4. The mothers who shared these stories believe that their lives were impacted by their Heavenly Father, who chose to step in when they needed help on their path.

A prompting or influencing event that causes us to change course can be as big as the decision to have another baby or as small as turning back to receive a phone call about a sick child. What they have in common is this: they are evidence that our Divine Parent is interested in our day-to-day lives. As Elder Lund has declared:

> He intervenes even in what we might think of as trivial matters. He is not some Divine Deity occasionally hurling cosmic thunderbolts at the earth from His throne on high. He is our Father, who intimately knows us and infinitely loves us, and who is not at all hesitant to use His limitless powers to bless and enrich and protect and direct us. In short, I firmly believe that if we have eyes

to see, we will learn that our Heavenly Father also watches over us "in every hour and in every moment" of our existence as well.[48]

Indeed, He watches over us constantly, and when needed, He will take the reins to ensure we stay on the path He knows is right for us.

Chapter 6
The Voice of Warning

MARY LYNNE had just sent her five-year-old daughter out the door to walk to her dance class down the street. After several minutes, this young mother climbed in the car to run some errands. As she slowly started to reverse the car out of her garage onto the snowy driveway, she heard a voice say, "Stop." Pausing momentarily, Mary Lynne looked around, confused. Seeing nothing, she continued to back out her car. She heard the voice again, louder now, saying, "Stop!" This time she parked the car and stepped outside to look around. That's when she found her daughter lying on the ground in the snow, under the car, between the wheels. Mary Lynne quickly enlisted a neighbor's help to pull the girl out from under the car. Besides being a bit frightened and cold, she was unharmed. If Mary Lynne had not stopped the car when she did, she would have turned the wheels to reverse out of her driveway. Her daughter likely would have been crushed.

Because Heavenly Father watches over us constantly, and because He loves us so dearly, He will occasionally warn us through the Spirit that we, or someone we love, is in danger. It seems important to note here that while the Spirit in some cases gives a warning that may help us avoid tragedy, that does not always happen. Myriad righteous parents have experienced tragedies without warning. We don't know why. What we do know is that we do not choose when we will receive revelation. Only God chooses that, according to His purposes, the scope of which only He truly understands. In a later chapter, I will discuss the topic of when the heavens seem silent. This chapter will focus on how the Spirit occasionally *does* give life-altering warnings if Heavenly Father chooses to communicate them and how we can be blessed if we are willing to listen.

The scriptures are full of examples when the Spirit has given a warning of impending trouble. God warned Joseph in a dream that Herod would seek to kill the baby Jesus and that he needed to take his family to Egypt (Matthew 2:13). The Apostle Paul "perceived" that if he were to leave with his crew to sail to Rome, they would be in danger. When the crew wanted to sail out anyway, Paul joined them only to later be shipwrecked and nearly killed (Acts 27:10–18). Lehi was warned in a dream that the people of Jerusalem would try to kill him and that the city would be destroyed (1 Nephi 2:1–2). Noah was warned that the earth would be destroyed because of the wickedness of man (Genesis 6:13).

These warnings from God are not just a thing of days past. He continues to warn his children in some circumstances when they are in need of protection. As modern-day Apostle Elder Richard G. Scott has declared, "On occasion, the Lord will give you an answer before you ask. This can occur when you are unaware of a danger or may be doing the wrong thing, mistakenly trusting that it is correct."[49] In this chapter are stories of mothers who have been warned by the Spirit for the safety and well-being of their children.

Laura had just picked up her son Carter from school to head to an afternoon dental appointment. She and Carter were talking while stopped at a red light. The light turned green, but as she started to pull out, Laura suddenly had a feeling that she needed to stop the car. "That's when I saw a car coming, and the woman driving was on her cell phone," Laura said. "She never made an attempt to stop but sped right through her red light. She would have T-boned us right on Carter's side of the car." Laura explained to her son that she was guided by the Spirit to stop the car. "I talked with him about following promptings when you get them, because they can sometimes save your life," she said. "We expressed our thanks for that prompting in our prayers that night." What a wise mother, who not only listened to a prompting but also took the opportunity to teach her son in that moment about the life-saving power of the Spirit.

Another mother shared with me how the Spirit gave her a prompting that likely saved her one-year-old daughter's life. Jen had put her baby, Sabrina, in a baby walker next to a Christmas decoration on the pantry door so she could play for a few minutes while Jen vacuumed upstairs. Here is what happened next:

> All of a sudden, I heard a voice saying, "Go to Sabrina." I thought, *Okay, I'll go check on her as soon as I'm done vacuuming up here.* Then I heard it again. Then I heard a loud, insistent voice almost yell, "Go to Sabrina!" It startled me so much that I instantly ran down the stairs without even turning off the vacuum. Sabrina was in her walker choking on a little jingle bell that she must have chewed off of the Christmas decoration. I would have not made it in time to save her if I hadn't listened to the urgent prompting of the Holy Ghost. By the time I finished vacuuming, it would have been too late. I'm so grateful for the Holy Ghost and can't believe it took three times for me to finally listen!

Another mother, Jenn, felt a warning sensation in the middle of a baseball game. "We were all talking and enjoying the game when my son was moved to a position he didn't normally play," Jenn said. "I immediately had an overwhelming feeling that this position would not be good for him. I became very aware of the game and felt that something was wrong." Moments later a ball was hit toward Carson, which popped up from the ground and hit him in the face. Carson fell to the ground. Jenn and her husband ran onto the field to find their son with a face unrecognizable from the swelling. In this case, Jenn's uneasy feeling didn't allow her to change the situation, but it was real evidence to her that Heavenly Father was aware of her and her son.

One mother shared how a prompting did help her intervene before her son was hurt. Melissa's son Jonathan was three years old, and for his birthday he got a small real hammer for a gift. "Jonathan was hammering something on the carpet, and I had a distinct feeling to get over to him," Melissa said. Her younger son, William, had just crawled over to sit with Jonathan. "I grabbed Jonathan's hand and stopped a hammer swing that would have hit William on the top of his head," she said. "William was not even one. I felt sick when I thought about what would have happened had I not received this prompting or had I not listened."

Sometimes we don't know exactly what kind of danger we have been guided to avert. One mother I spoke with was prompted by the Spirit to remove her son from a compromising situation. Her son was dating a girl whose parents were getting a divorce, and she was understandably upset. It was late at night, and he wasn't home yet. "I had a feeling that I needed to go get him," the young man's mother said. "I found them all snuggled up together in a car as he was comforting her. I knocked on the window and said, 'You need to come home.' That was hard." This mother will never know what might have happened if she hadn't followed her prompting to go get her son. What she does know is that the Spirit was directing her that night.

Each of these mothers described the warnings they received in terms of a sudden feeling that something wasn't right or that they needed to go check on a child. They hadn't necessarily been asking for inspiration in the moment, but Heavenly Father felt it important to send a signal. My friend Julie described the warning feelings she has received as knots in her stomach or being unable to sleep. On one occasion, her son Eli came home asking to play at a friend's house. For reasons unknown to her, Julie instantly got a tight, uncomfortable feeling in her stomach. "I have sent Eli home with friends on numerous occasions," Julie said, "but this time was different. I told Eli about my feelings. He was defiant at first, but soon realized that this was a real feeling and shouldn't be ignored. We have since only had this friend at our home to play, but I believe those sickening feelings were there for a reason." Again, we may not always know why the Spirit prompts us to act one way or another, but we can feel confident that we are better off following that counsel.

Julie has had the same feeling other times when the warning's purpose has been more clear. As she explained, "On other occasions my stomach has instantly felt upset when thinking about a child. Then I have found my toddler headed to the street or already in the street. Or I have come into a room in the middle of the night to find a blanket wrapped around my child's head." Julie is in tune enough to know when Heavenly Father is prompting her to help one of her children out of danger, and she is willing to act on those promptings.

We are given a promise in the scriptures that "if ye will enter in by the way, and receive the Holy Ghost, it will show unto you all things what ye should do" (2 Nephi 32:5). Heavenly Father is aware of everything that is happening in our lives. He won't stop every pain or every trial, because life, after all, is a test. But at times He will choose to show us what we need to do to keep our family safe through a voice of warning. If we are constantly listening for that voice, we will have opportunities to bless, and sometimes even rescue, our children.

Chapter 7

The Role of the Comforter

WHEN CHRIST was on the earth, His disciples and members of the Church could see Him, follow Him, hear His voice, and find comfort in His words. The thought of losing their beloved Savior must have been almost too much to bear. But Christ was not going to leave them alone. He promised them this: "I will pray the Father, and he shall give you another Comforter, that he may abide with you for ever. . . . Ye know him; for he dwelleth with you, and shall be in you. I will not leave you comfortless" (John 14: 16–18). Christ was promising His people that He would leave them with the constantly accessible comfort of the Holy Ghost. What a beautiful promise for all who would embrace this gift.

As mothers, we have plenty of opportunities for worry, heartache, and occasionally pain, whether brought on by decisions of our children or circumstances outside of anyone's control. We know we can count on the hard times—after all, life is a test, and most things that bring great joy seem to come with at least a bit of struggle, suffering, or sacrifice. We also know, however, that our Father in Heaven has not left us alone to handle our heartaches. In this chapter are stories from mothers who can testify of how they have been comforted in times of trial.

One mother I greatly admire went through an experience where she nearly died in a hospital room due to severe internal bleeding. Recently, she let me read her journal about the experience. In that journal, she recorded how she was lying on the hospital room bed in great fear that she wouldn't make it to see her oldest daughter have children or see her youngest daughter get married. She prayed for comfort and strength. She recorded in her journal her experience of momentarily being outside her body, looking down on the room. She wrote, "I looked over to the side of the room, and I imagined . . ." Then she had stopped writing, and she crossed out the word *imagined*. She continued with the words, "I saw my Savior."

This isn't doctrine. No one can ever know for sure what happened that night or who was in this mother's hospital room while she fought for her life. But it is her testimony that the Savior was there for her in her hour of suffering. Her fear was removed in that moment, and she was filled with peace.

Thankfully, this mother was able to make a full recovery and is now able to find joy in her children and grandchildren. Hearing her story brought to mind one of my favorite poems. The poem by Mary Stevenson, titled "Footprints in the Sand," captures the story of a woman who had a dream one night in which she was walking with her Savior while scenes from her life flashed across the sky. The woman noticed footprints in the sand while each scene played. She began to feel uneasy when she noticed that during many times in her life there were two sets of footprints, but during her most difficult times there were only one set of footprints. Thinking she had been left alone during those periods of struggle, the woman inquired why. In the poem, the Lord responds with:

> "The times when you have
> seen only one set of footprints,
> is when I carried you."

I love the image of our Savior lifting us up in our times of greatest trial. Christ may not physically be with us in each circumstance of struggle, but the Holy Spirit can be. That was Christ's promise when He left the earth: we would not be left comfortless.

My friend Jenn had a clear opportunity to feel the comforting power of the Spirit during a pregnancy with her fourth child. During this pregnancy, Jenn was busy taking care of her three other children and actively participating in her calling as a counselor in the Relief Society. Her pregnancy was noticeably different from her other three. "Unlike my other pregnancies," she said, "I was very calm and patient. I seemed to be able to do everything that I needed to get done without getting frazzled. I felt very in tune with the Spirit and felt a great outpouring of love for my three children." The Spirit may have been strengthening Jenn, preparing her for the tragedy that was coming.

Twenty-one weeks into her pregnancy, Jenn found out that the baby she was carrying had died. She not only felt the Spirit particularly strongly before this occurred, but she also felt the comfort she needed so much afterward. As she explained, "I feel that I was so in tune with the Spirit during this time to help me feel spiritually strong for the delivery, recovery, and loss I went through."

I can't imagine all that this mother suffered. But her testimony is a reminder to me of the great blessing of the Comforter and the peace to which we constantly have access.

Sometimes the Spirit comes to strengthen us when we are going through physical pain. My friend Angie shared with me how she felt the powerful presence of the Spirit as she was about to give birth to her first child. Before heading to the hospital, she asked for a blessing of strength from her husband and her brother-in-law. "At the very moment I made the request," Angie explained, "I was overcome with such physical strength, spiritual vision, and a calming spirit. It was a direct gift from God." Even while going through the pain of childbirth, she continued to feel the Spirit with her:

> I remember actually feeling the comfort and the calming presence of the Holy Ghost during Sam's delivery. Heavenly Father answered my prayers and truly sent comforting angels to my bedside. I also felt overwhelmed by the responsibility, and I felt overwhelmed by the anticipated delivery of my baby. As I turned to

the Lord for physical help, wisdom, and comfort, I was blessed beyond what I could have imagined. I know that if we just remember to ask Him, we can feel of His Spirit, and He will comfort and strengthen us.

What a beautiful testimony of the Comforter's ability to strengthen us whenever we feel weak, scared, or hurt. I too have felt the powerful presence of the Spirit when I have been in the delivery room with a new baby. Even though my body had experienced the intense physical pain of childbirth, the second each child was put into my arms, I was overwhelmed with peace, strength, and love.

The Comforter can also play a role when we are worried about our children—something I think mothers (myself included) have quite a knack for. One mother shared with me how the Spirit helped her feel physical relief from the sickening worry she felt when her son was late returning home. Carla's son had taken a bus ride with friends to see the Manti pageant—a historical play that was taking place about two hours away. She knew he would arrive home late, but Carla's son still wasn't back well past when he should have been. (This was at a time before teenagers carried around their own cell phones.) Carla started feeling sick with worry and concern for her son, not knowing where he was or what might have happened to him. So she decided to get out of bed and pray. "I was totally upset before that prayer," she explained. "But after praying, I got back in bed and the feeling was totally gone. This whole calmness filled my stomach. I actually moved my hands around my stomach and looked for the sick feelings. And they were completely gone."

Shortly after, her son came in the door and explained that the bus had gotten a flat tire. Looking back on the experience, what stands out to Carla was how literal the removal of her suffering was. As she said, "I'll never forget that feeling of knowing your pain and then having it taken away. It's just a fact that when I reached a point when I couldn't cope, I needed to ask for help. It was a complete, instant removal of suffering. I'll always remember that."

That same mother had another experience, this time with her daughter, where she so directly felt the comfort of the Spirit. Carla's daughter, Stephy, was pregnant and assigned to bed rest for eleven weeks. Carla asked Stephy if she would like to stay with her for a while to get a change of scenery. One night, though she was still quite early in her pregnancy, Stephy's water broke, and she started hemorrhaging. "Blood was everywhere," Carla recalled. "We got in the car and booked it to the hospital." Luckily the doctor had decided to come to work early that night and was ready to help in the delivery. With so many weeks still remaining to her due date, things were looking dire. All Carla could do was wait.

"About an hour later, the nurse came out and said both mother and baby had survived," Carla said. "But the doctor then explained that there was blood in the baby's brain ventricles." That could mean lasting complications. The whole night was a tangle of raw emotions. "I was so sad I didn't know what to do," she said. Stephy, trying to find comfort, reached into a drawer and pulled out the Bible that was waiting inside. Flipping it open to a random page, she read the first scripture she saw, which was John 14:1: "Let not your heart be troubled: ye believe in God, believe also in me."

It seemed that scripture was a direct answer to the prayers of two mothers who needed comfort. Heavenly Father was directing a mother and grandmother to just the message they needed in that moment. They needed to believe that all would be well—something God already knew. Carla wrote out the scripture and put it on her dashboard as a reminder to "let not [her] heart be troubled." She also started singing the hymn "Count Your Many Blessings" as she drove to and from the hospital. That song, she told me, brought the Spirit to strengthen her in that dark hour. She testified, "By the time I got back to the hospital, the sun was shining, and I knew without a doubt that I had been comforted by that song and scripture."

Heidi Poelman

The Spirit is also available constantly to comfort our children in their times of pain and anguish. My friend Jenn, whom I mentioned previously, shared with me an experience when her daughter found peace and strength after a family tragedy. Jenn's sister, Amber, had passed away unexpectedly. Amber had been a beloved aunt to Jenn's oldest daughter, Annie, who was only four at the time. Aunt Amber had promised to take Annie swimming, and for months Annie woke up upset, realizing that it would never happen. "We would talk about the power of prayer to help her sleep," Jenn said. "It broke my heart to see my sweet daughter so sad. During this time, I found myself often praying that Annie would get back to her happy self. I found great comfort through the Spirit that she would once again be as happy as she was, and even more so."

Eventually, Annie's nightly waking and crying came to a stop. Looking back on the experience, Jenn says, "The blessings I was promised through the Spirit have come to fruition. At almost eight years old now, our Annie is full of joy." Not only did Jenn find comfort in knowing that Annie would eventually recover, but also Annie was able to find peace, even at her young age and after an experience of such deep loss. Heavenly Father was not going to let mother or daughter suffer alone.

Another mother received a blessing of peace when her son was dealing with recurring night terrors. On the nights when he was home, the boy's father would give their son a blessing to help him relax and go back to sleep. But because he traveled frequently, the father wasn't always home. On those nights, when her son would wake up, this mother would ask her son to kneel beside her in prayer. Afterward, she would give him a hug and ask, "How are you?" He would regularly say, "I can go back to bed now." He was a teenager at the time, and according to his mother, "He was so frightened, and yet, all that would disappear the minute we'd start to pray." What a powerful reminder of the quickest, surest go-to solution for helping our children when they are hurting or afraid.

Sometimes, we as mothers need strength just to get through the day during those inevitably frustrating moments. I love a promise from President Ezra Taft Benson, who explained how the Holy Ghost can strengthen us and prepare us to be the best mothers we can be to our children. He said, "The Holy Ghost causes our feelings to be more tender. We feel more charitable and compassionate. We are calmer. We have greater capacity to love."[50]

I know what I need most sometimes is just a greater capacity to love and be patient with my children when things aren't going so smoothly around the house—say, when someone just colored with markers on the wall (again), or someone left toothpaste all over the sink (again), or the kids are squabbling over a toy (again), or someone doesn't want to practice piano (again). I am grateful to know that, if I am prayerful, I can rely on the Holy Ghost to give me that greater compassion and greater capacity to love when I need it. I love what my neighbor said helps her to access that power: "A lot of times when I'm frustrated with my kids, I'll say a silent prayer to help me not only calm down but to know what they need at that moment. I've learned time after time that when kids are the least lovable, they need love the most." Indeed they do. And when they need love and we aren't feeling very loving, it's the Holy Ghost who can get us there.

Sometimes, as mothers, what we need most is an ability to feel loved and important ourselves when we so often go without the accolades of the world. I don't know of anyone who has a better perspective on this than my friend Julie, whose husband travels the world, receiving standing ovations on a regular basis while she holds down the fort at home. The Spirit found a way to let her know how important her job was, even without nightly praise:

> For the last three years, my husband has traveled the globe as a well-known musician. When this group began, I found out I was pregnant with my fourth. The Piano Guys had to pay their dues and perform two to three weeks out of the month all across the world. For the next two years, I had a rough pregnancy, had a baby, then received no sleep for the next year it seems due to her

infant stages and constant wakings. I was being torn apart physically and emotionally by the rest of my children . . . receiving no praise or thanks at the end of the day. All this while my husband was receiving praise and accolades, traveling the world, eating and sleeping in five-star hotels, and receiving standing ovations every night. This was a low time in my life. I am a strong, independent woman, but this did me in.

One night I received an email from a mother who wrote to me, specifically thanking me for my sacrifice and telling me that she was ready to end her life until she came across the music of the Piano Guys and how their joy and faith shone through their music. It has since kept her going, encouraged her to seek out the Church, and uplifted her spirit to follow her dreams. I was instantly immersed in the Spirit and knew that all this sacrifice was worth it completely. The Spirit has helped me to keep a positive outlook since then. It was when reading that letter that the statement "No other success can compensate for failure in the home" really took meaning. I am proud to call myself a full-time mommy!

At times, all we really need is a reminder that we are not raising these children alone. Our Father in Heaven will strengthen us and bring us peace in our times of trial and pain. He has even promised to be with us during those dark hours. He said, "Fear thou not; for I am with thee: be not dismayed; for I am thy God: I will strengthen thee; yea, I will help thee; yea, I will uphold thee with the right hand of my righteousness. . . . For I the Lord thy God will hold thy right hand, saying unto thee, Fear not; I will help thee" (Isaiah 41:10, 13). What a beautiful promise to keep tucked in our hearts when they are aching: He is always there.

Chapter 8

God's Power on Earth

How the Priesthood Blesses Mothers

ONE DAY in February 2002, Sarah, a mother of two, started feeling sick. Her heart was racing, and she felt dizzy and light-headed. The next day, she felt worse. She got to the point where she felt like she was going to pass out. Knowing something was wrong, Sarah drove to an urgent care center, where the doctor did a stress test and an EKG. The tests confirmed that her heart was racing, but the doctor didn't seem worried. He sent her home and asked her to follow up with her own doctor in a few days.

By the next day, her symptoms had worsened. Sarah went to another doctor who, after examining her, said she had signs of anxiety. As the doctor explained, heightened anxiety wasn't uncommon with the security concerns surrounding the 2002 Salt Lake City Olympics. Like the previous day, this doctor sent her home.

Confused and frustrated, Sarah wondered what to do next. She decided to ask her neighbor John for a priesthood blessing. In that blessing, John was inspired to tell Sarah exactly what she needed to hear. This is what she wrote in her journal about the blessing she received that day: "I am grateful for the priesthood and for the blessing I received. In that blessing, I was told to trust my instincts. Because of that, I went back to the doctor for the third time in four days." Her decision to trust her instincts would ultimately save her life.

Again at the doctor's office, Sarah tried to explain that something more than anxiety was affecting her. She knew it. "I lay on the exam table and cried because I knew there was something very wrong and nobody would believe me," she wrote of the experience. "My doctor bought into the anxiety thing. I heard her and the others talking about it outside my door." As she sat helplessly waiting, Sarah recalled her blessing to trust her instincts. She gathered her confidence, partly which came with her thirty years of medical experience working as a registered nurse. When the doctor came back, Sarah asked for the only thing that came to mind: a blood test. The doctor agreed and drew blood for the test. "Shortly thereafter," Sarah explained, "the doctor called me and said my hematocrit [red blood cell count] was dangerously low and that I needed to get to the hospital to receive blood." She left right away. After being examined at the hospital, doctors discovered that Sarah had severe internal bleeding in her stomach. If she had waited another day, she likely would have died.

Without the message in her blessing that she needed to trust her instincts, this mother may have simply believed what the doctors had to say, that she was suffering from anxiety and should stay home to rest. If she had done that, the consequences would have been tragic.

Priesthood blessings are one channel that Heavenly Father uses to communicate with us and give us the strength and power we need as we navigate this mortal journey. The priesthood, as Joseph F. Smith defined, is "the power of God delegated to man by which man can act in the earth for the salvation of the human family."[51] Priesthood blessings, and the ability to feel prompted to call upon their power, are available to each of us as a way to bless and strengthen our families.

As mothers, we are in a unique position to be aware of the needs of our family. We are called as nurturers, teachers, and cocreators with our eternal God as we raise our children. As women and mothers, we do not have the authority to administer priesthood blessings, but we do have every opportunity to call upon and be blessed by that power at any time we stand in need. The Spirit can direct us at any time to request a blessing, and through those blessings, God communicates with His children. As Elder Neil L. Anderson of the Quorum of the Twelve Apostles explained, "The blessings of the priesthood are infinitely greater than the one who is asked to administer the gift. To receive the blessings, power, and promises of the priesthood in this life and the next is one of the great opportunities and responsibilities of mortality."[52] That notion stands out to me: to *receive* these blessings is one of the great responsibilities of our life on earth. As mothers, we are in the position to help our children do just that.

Beyond the personal blessings available through the priesthood, mothers also have access to "keys of knowledge and power." Indeed, as Joseph Smith surmised in a Relief Society meeting in 1842, for sisters who have been endowed in the temple, the keys of knowledge and power become available to them in the very same way that they are available to men.[53] As well-renowned author, publisher, Church leader, and Deseret Book CEO and president Sheri Dew puts it, "These keys provide access to heaven—to godly power, to personal revelation, and to heavenly help."[54] She goes on to emphasize that "*all* of us, covenant men and women alike, receive the gift and power of the Holy Ghost [through the priesthood]. We may *all* speak and lead as directed by the Spirit, receive and understand the mysteries of the kingdom, and learn to open the heavens."[55] That promise and understanding is comforting to me as I consider how the priesthood can bless me as a mother and bless my children too.

In short, mothers have the right to every blessing our Father in Heaven has to offer through His power on earth. What beautiful promises we have been given, if we can only remember to seek them in our lives. What we must constantly ask ourselves is, "Am I utilizing the great power that is available to me?" In this chapter are stories of mothers who have called upon priesthood power to bless their homes and families.

Laura had three children in elementary school when her sister decided to travel to Russia to adopt a child. Her sister asked Laura to accompany her while she traveled, which meant that Laura would be away from her family for a month. Anxious about leaving her husband and children for that long but wanting to support her sister, Laura wasn't sure what to do. So she turned to her husband for a priesthood blessing. Laura said that during the blessing, "Almost immediately I felt a peace come over me that all would be well at home and that helping my sister was the right thing to do." Heavenly Father had guided her decision through a blessing. She packed up her things and said good-bye to her family. Looking back, Laura is glad she was guided to make that choice at the time, even though it was a difficult one. "Yes, we missed each other," she said, "but my experiences in Russia were so eye opening, and the family realized Mom does a lot at home."

This mother recognizes and values the priesthood power in her home and utilizes it for herself and her children regularly. As she says, "Before a surgery, school year, or important event or test, or during a serious illness, the kids will get a blessing from Alan [her husband, the kids' father]. Sometimes they will ask for it or he will offer to give it if they would like it. It's a wonderful blessing to have the priesthood in our home, and I want my sons and daughter to recognize this great gift."

Like many families, we also have a tradition of giving annual priesthood blessings before our children go off to start another year of school. We did this recently when our son was preparing to enter third grade, our daughter first grade, and our other daughter her second year of preschool. As my husband gave the blessings to each child, I was aware of the powerful feeling in the room. Our children were privileged to hear their father as he placed his hands on their heads and gave them a blessing of health, happiness, courage, and anything else they had specifically asked for. To me, these regular blessings present an opportunity to show our Father in Heaven that we are turning to Him for guidance and strength in everything that we do. The action serves as an important reminder that we are in a partnership with our Father in Heaven to raise these children.

Setting the expectation that children have access to priesthood blessings any time they need is a powerful tool for them. I love how my mother-in-law, Kerry, expresses her appreciation for that gift when she was raising her children: "It's so cool to have a father in your home who is worthy of the priesthood," she said. "We'd ask for blessings about school, missions, or struggles. It's a natural thing to use the resources in your home. I have felt prompted to ask my children if they would like a blessing. It might provide guidance, something solid they could take spiritually. It was something I valued. I wanted them to have faith in priesthood blessings and to know that during any struggle they could ask for a blessing."

What stands out to me in Kerry's words is not only how much she appreciates the power in her home but also how she has followed promptings to ask her children if they would like a blessing. Again, as mothers we are sometimes in the best spot to feel guidance about what our children need. As we choose to rely on the priesthood, we teach our children about accessing that power as well. As my friend JaKell said, "I have felt prompted to ask for priesthood blessings whenever my children are sick or in need of uplift, and I think this is doing them a great service, because they are starting to understand that they can draw upon Heavenly Father's power too."

My friend Julie recognizes the importance of teaching her children to have a special reverence and appreciation for the priesthood from the time they are small. "They are not struggling with big issues yet," she said, "but helping them get into the habit of asking Dad for a blessing before school begins or when they feel very ill is a great start. We teach them that priesthood blessings are extra special. They even get to sit on the 'special chair' and be in the 'special room' with us."

Not only does Julie teach her children how they can utilize the priesthood in their lives, but she is also an example of doing the same. As she says, "I can't even count how many times I have asked for a priesthood blessing concerning my role as a mother. For me, it's about receiving the strength to keep going!"

One mother, Carla, helps her boys appreciate the priesthood power by encouraging a priesthood meeting tradition with the other men in the family. She said, "Our kids knew from the time they were twelve that they would attend [the semiannual general] priesthood meeting with their dads and uncles. Then they would meet up somewhere and all share their thoughts about the meeting. Rick [their dad] always said each meeting was the best meeting ever. Their attitude was always that it was special. The kids now have that tradition." By teaching them to honor and appreciate the priesthood when they were small, this mother helped her boys create an enduring legacy. Her adult sons now still honor the priesthood power.

The priesthood can also be a powerful source of strength and healing for mothers and their children. One mother, Janis, shared with me how a priesthood blessing helped her support her son on the day he was leaving for the missionary training center. The morning her son Shawn was heading to the MTC, Janis had to have mouth surgery for a root canal that had gone bad. She had had this type of surgery before, usually with a lot of pain and swelling. Concerned that she wouldn't be able to give her son the support he needed, Janis asked for a priesthood blessing. "Jay gave me a blessing at 8:00 a.m." she said. Afterward, she realized "there was no pain and no swelling. I was able to go and be with my son that day." Janis's willingness to rely on the priesthood helped her have the strength to be the mother she needed to be for her son.

Another mother, Diana, shared with me how one night their youngest son was suffering from a severe earache. The pain continued for her little four-year-old even after taking the medication that typically helped. "After seeing him cry in such pain all through the night," Diana said, "I asked him if he wanted Daddy to give him a priesthood blessing." Her son said yes, and shortly after his father administered the blessing, their son went peacefully to sleep. Diana remembers the night well as a powerful witness of her Heavenly Father's love:

> The memory is still vivid in our minds of the joy we felt as parents from witnessing the power of the priesthood and the blessing it was to see an almost instantaneous relief from the physical pain our son had been experiencing. For me, as a mother, it was an occasion to express deep gratitude to my Father in Heaven for the blessing of having a husband and a father to our children who, at a moment's notice, was worthy to use his priesthood to bless our family.

Diana was the one to ask her son if he would like a blessing from his father. As mothers, we have a vital role to play in influencing how the priesthood is used and respected in our home. My friend Melissa shared with me how she was able to help her husband appreciate the variety of ways their family could utilize his ability to administer the priesthood. In her home growing up, Melissa's parents taught that their children could ask for a blessing anytime they needed one, whether the issue seemed big or small. Melissa's husband, Greg, grew up using the priesthood more sparingly. As she explained:

> Greg had the priesthood in his home, but in his home growing up it was used for going back to school and for extreme issues. I remember one of the first times I asked him to give Jonathan a blessing, he didn't think it was necessary because it was a rather small problem. I expressed my feelings on the power of priesthood blessings. I feel it is there should we feel prompted to ask for it or if we need it, whatever the issue may be. (That being said, I feel that it shouldn't be abused, because it is a sacred thing.) He said he had never thought about it that way.

Now, as the priesthood bearer in their home, Greg is happy to give blessings whenever he or his wife or any of his children feel one is needed. Melissa was able to be a great influence by sharing her testimony that the priesthood is available for us to access at any time.

As mothers, we are in a distinct position to understand what our families need. If we are listening, we can hear when our Father in Heaven is whispering to us through His Spirit. He will let us know when we or one of our children could use the healing or comforting power of a priesthood blessing. We are granted access to that power. What does that mean for us as women and mothers? As Sheri Dew put it, "It means that we can receive revelation, be blessed and aided by the ministering of angels, learn to part the veil that separates us from our Heavenly Father, be strengthened to resist temptation, be protected, and be enlightened and made smarter than we are."[56] In short, if we choose to access it, we can have God's power to bring us and our children closer to Him anytime we choose.

All the blessings of heaven can be ours when we choose to receive the priesthood power in our lives. We are promised this much in the scriptures: "And also all they who receive this priesthood receive me, saith the Lord; for he that receiveth my servants receiveth me; and he that receiveth me receiveth my Father; and he that receiveth my Father receiveth my Father's kingdom; therefore all that my Father hath shall be given unto him" (D&C 84:35–38). Keep in mind that the word *receive* can mean to come into possession of as well as to welcome, to accept as true, or to believe.[57] In other words, the Lord Himself has promised us that if we *receive* (believe, welcome, accept) the priesthood in our lives, then we can have all that the Father has. As mothers, are we appreciating and utilizing this power in our lives? If so, then we are welcoming the blessings of heaven into our home. That is God's promise.

Chapter 9

Angels among Us

WHILE WRITING this book, I interviewed several women about how they felt spiritual support as they raised their children. Something that came up frequently, which I was not expecting, was the topic of angels. At first, I wasn't sure the subject fit into my focus on how we can be guided and comforted through the Spirit. But then I came across a scripture in 2 Nephi that caught my attention. Here Nephi is teaching the means by which angels communicate with us on earth. He said, "Angels speak *by the power of the Holy Ghost*; wherefore, they speak the words of Christ. Wherefore, I said unto you, feast upon the words of Christ; for behold, the words of Christ will tell you all things what ye should do" (32:3, italics added). The way angels guide and communicate with us, like our Father in Heaven, is through the Spirit. With that in mind, I decided to explore the role of angels in guiding us as mothers.

Angels are a rich part of our scriptural history. As Elder Lund stated, "There are 543 references to angels in the four standard works, and more than a hundred more in Joseph Smith's *History of the Church*."[58] Here are just a few examples:

- Within days of leaving the Garden, God sent an angel to teach Adam and Eve the meaning of sacrifice (Moses 5:6–8).

Heidi Poelman

- An angel stopped Abraham from sacrificing his son Isaac (Genesis 22:11–12).
- Daniel declares that he was protected in the lions' den because God sent an angel to close the lions' mouths (Daniel 6:22).
- An angel visited Mary and Joseph to announce the coming birth of the Savior (Luke 1:26–37; Matthew 1:20).
- An angel announced the birth of Jesus to the shepherds, and a host of angels sang that night to celebrate His coming to the world (Luke 2:9–14).
- An angel warned Joseph that the baby Jesus was in danger from King Herod and that the family needed to flee to Egypt (Matthew 2:13–15).
- Angels ministered to Christ after He was tempted by Satan in the wilderness (Matthew 4:11).
- An angel appeared to strengthen Christ while He suffered in Gethsemane (Luke 22:43).
- Angels were with Christ as He ministered to the Nephites (3 Nephi 17:24).
- Angel Moroni visited with Joseph Smith multiple times about the Book of Mormon (Joseph Smith—History 1).

Should we believe that angels are only a part of ancient religious history or only relevant for prophets and people who will have some major impact on the world? Not at all. Consider what modern-day Apostle Elder Jeffrey R. Holland has to say about the matter: "Usually such beings are not seen. Sometimes they are. But seen or unseen *they are always near.* Sometimes their assignments are very grand and have significance for the whole world. Sometimes the messages are more private. Occasionally the angelic purpose is to warn. But most often it is to comfort, to provide some form of merciful attention, guidance in difficult times."[59]

Angels are *always* near. And based on the experiences people shared with me, it seems possible that the angels sent to minister to us often have a personal connection. Consider the story of my neighbor Janis, whose mother and father have both passed away. Janis was planning to go to the temple on Tuesday, just like she had for years, when she felt a strange prompting that she should wait and go on Thursday. She didn't know why, but that week she followed the feeling and waited.

On Thursday, Janis arrived at the temple with some family names. She had recently had surgery, so she was unable to do the baptisms herself. She decided to look around for a youth who could do the baptisms for her that day, but everyone she asked had their own family names to work on. Discouraged, Janis decided to head upstairs and find some other work to do. That's when she heard her mother's voice in her mind. "Go back downstairs," the voice told her. So she turned around and headed back to the baptism area. To her surprise, Janis found her niece waiting there to do baptisms. "I asked if she had any names with her," said Janis, "and she didn't." Janis's niece, along with her cousin who happened to be there, were able to take care of Janis's family names.

Janis wasn't the only one who sensed her mother's presence that day. Her sister, who also happened to be in the temple, told Janis that she had felt their mom and dad at the temple. Their other sister, Brenda, had been out walking on the same day when she had a similar feeling. As Janis explained, "Brenda was getting married soon and was nervous about it. She said she heard Mom talking to her in her mind, telling her, 'It's going to be okay.'" On the same day, three sisters felt the presence of their parents guiding and comforting them from beyond the veil. Their angels were with them.

Janis has had other experiences where she's felt her mom has been in touch to provide direction or strength. One time, a daughter had broken up with a boyfriend who was sending threatening texts. Janis was worrying about her safety when, as she explains, "I was praying, and Mom said to me, 'We are watching over her, and it's going to be okay.' They are watching our every move."

Another neighbor shared with me an experience when a deceased grandmother was able to provide messages of comfort from beyond the veil during an important transition in life. Pattie's daughter had just graduated from college and was moving to San Francisco to start her career. Pattie and her husband asked their daughter's permission to give her a father's blessing to help give her strength in this new city. As he was giving the blessing, "an acute message that her great-grandmother would be a guardian angel watching over her distinctly came to him," Pattie said. "He didn't say anything at first, and later he told me that he felt a bit overwhelmed. As he quietly went out to the car to get a few more boxes to unload, he told me he prayed once again to know if what he had been told was right. It came at him again, that same intensity of message as strong as before."

Pattie expressed to her husband that she wouldn't be surprised if the message really had been a communication from the great-grandmother, since Pattie had been worried about their daughter's move, and the message would be an answer to prayer. "So we both got into the car and prayed in the middle of the mission district of San Francisco for verification," Pattie said. "The message hit both of us. I think my grandmother was telling me to believe it and get on with it. She was a strong-minded woman." When Pattie and her husband told their daughter about the message they had received, they learned that their daughter had picked up on similar feelings from her great-grandmother as well. So during this experience, three people had sensed that a beloved family member had been in touch from beyond the veil to provide strength and comfort.

Another friend told me of a time when her family was fasting and praying for a child. As she said, "When our answer came, there was no doubt in our minds that it was helped along by a family member from beyond the veil." Should we really be surprised that Heavenly Father is willing to send along angels, even our own family members, when we are in need? Or that, perhaps, our departed family members are granted access by our Heavenly Father to communicate with us whenever they feel they should because they love us? As our first modern-day prophet, Joseph

Smith, testified, "If you live up to your privilege, the angels cannot be restrained from being your associates."[60] What a comforting promise to know that if we are living worthily, the angels who so desire to attend to us cannot be restrained. That is our privilege.

That privilege may become most meaningful to remember when we are going through the inevitable trials of mortality. Perhaps one of the most difficult times in our religious history was experienced by the early Saints, who gave up nearly everything they owned to follow a prophet's call. They crossed the plains in blistering heat and freezing snow to reach a safe haven where they could worship with their families. These heroic pioneers suffered through unimaginable tragedies, including severe physical hardship and the emotional pain of losing loved ones along the way.

Despite the hardships, their testimonies of their God and their cause stood firm. I love the testimony of one of these pioneers, a member of the Martin Handcart Company, who asserts that during these most difficult times, God did not leave them alone: "I have pulled my handcart when I was so weak and weary from illness and lack of food that I could hardly put one foot ahead of the other. . . . I have gone on [only to realize] the cart began pushing me. I have looked back many times to see who was pushing my cart, but my eyes saw no one. I knew then that the angels of God were there."[61]

Our Father in Heaven is willing to send comforting angels in our times of struggle, whether we are aware of their presence or not. Mormon once asked this of his son, Moroni, "Has the day of miracles ceased? Or have angels ceased to appear unto the children of men? Or has he withheld the power of the Holy Ghost from them? Or will he, so long as time shall last, or the earth shall stand, or there shall be one man upon the face thereof to be saved? Behold I say unto you, Nay; for . . . it is by faith that angels appear and minister unto men" (Moroni 7:35–37). Moroni said that angels "are subject unto [Christ], to minister according to the word of his command, showing themselves unto them of strong faith and a firm mind in every form of godliness" (verse 30).

Heidi Poelman

The day of miracles had not ceased then, nor has it ceased now. Through the power of the Holy Ghost, as long as we are faithful, we are promised that we can have the comforting and guiding power of angels in our lives. As Christ Himself promised, "I will go before your face. I will be on your right hand and on your left, and my Spirit shall be in your hearts, and mine angels round about you, to bear you up" (D&C 84:88). As a mother, it is a blessing to know that on those days when my strength, my faith, my patience, or my courage is being tested to the limits, heaven's angels might just be there with me.

Chapter 10

Nearer My God to Thee

Strengthening Our Ability to Hear

OUR FATHER in Heaven loves us deeply and wants to be in touch with us to guide us, to warn us, and to comfort us in times of need. He loves His children. He wants to lead us along. He wants to guide us as we pursue our parenting partnership with Him. But this communication channel is not a one-way deal. He is there, and we need to be there too. He expects us to reach out to Him and to listen as He communicates with us through His Spirit. If we want to be in touch with our Heavenly Father in our day-to-day lives, we have to want it, we have to work for it, and we have to have faith as we wait for His voice. We are promised over and over again that if we seek, we shall find. Like the image of Christ standing at the door without a handle, if we want the Spirit in our lives, we have to open the door and let Him in.

Faith and Desire

So much of our spiritual sensitivity boils down to one very important thing: our faith. Faith, as we read in the scriptures, is "the substance of things hoped for, the evidence of things not seen" (Hebrews 11:1). Faith is rooted in a desire for something and a belief in the possibility of attaining it. But faith is more than belief. As President James E. Talmage explained, "Belief, in one of its accepted senses, may consist in a merely intellectual assent, while faith implies such confidence and conviction as will impel to action. . . . Belief is in a sense passive, an agreement or acceptance only; faith is active and positive, embracing such reliance and confidence as will lead to works."[62] If we want to have the Spirit guiding our lives, we need to believe so much that we are willing to act, to show our willingness to have it. How much do we want that influence? How are we showing our Heavenly Father?

After Christ came to visit the Nephites and set apart twelve disciples to lead the Church, those twelve had an opportunity to demonstrate their desire for the Spirit to be among them. We read in 3 Nephi that "the twelve did teach the multitude; and behold, they did cause that the multitude should kneel down upon the face of the earth, and should pray unto the Father in the name of Jesus. . . . And they did pray for that which they most desired; and they desired that the Holy Ghost should be given unto them" (19:6, 9). The Holy Ghost is what they *most* desired. Therefore, they were willing to kneel down and ask.

Elder David A. Bednar asked this question: "Do we likewise remember to pray earnestly and consistently for that which we should most desire, even the Holy Ghost? Or do we become distracted by the cares of the world and the routine of daily living and take for granted or even neglect this most valuable of all gifts? Receiving the Holy Ghost starts with our sincere and constant desire for His companionship in our lives."[63]

We can have a direct impact on whether we enjoy the presence of the Spirit in our lives. If we have a great desire for it, and if we have the faith that it can happen, then we are well on our way to receiving guidance and comfort from our Father in Heaven. Elder Boyd K. Packer put it simply when he said, "The flow of revelation depends on your faith. You exercise faith by causing, or by making, your mind accept or believe as truth that which *you* cannot, by reason alone, prove for certainty."[64] We cannot prove the presence of the Spirit in our lives. What we can do is want it, hope for it, and do everything in our power to be worthy of it. Then we may be the recipients of the same great blessing that the Lord once promised Enos: "I will grant unto thee according to thy desires, because of thy faith" (Enos 1:12).

Obedience

We can be worthy of having the Spirit in our lives only if we are being obedient to the commandments our Heavenly Father has given us. The Spirit cannot dwell in darkness. We are given a simple promise in the Doctrine and Covenants: "And no man receiveth a fulness unless he keepeth his commandments. He that keepeth his commandments receiveth truth and light, until he is glorified in truth and knoweth all things" (93:27–28). If we want to receive light and truth, we must prove our worthiness through obedience.

Elder James E. Faust expanded on that promise, noting that if we are worthy, we can have "an ample shield against the power of Lucifer and his hosts." He explains, "This protection lies in the spirit of discernment through the gift of the Holy Ghost. This gift comes undeviatingly by personal revelation to those who strive to obey the commandments of the Lord and to follow the counsel of the living prophets."[65] If we are obedient, we can have the privilege of being able to see good and evil clearly, even having the "gift of discernment" to guide us in our daily choices. What mother wouldn't benefit from that as she makes ongoing decisions about how to best raise her children?

Part of being worthy of qualifying for the Spirit is taking care of our inner vessel. Beyond choosing the right in our deeds and actions, we must have virtuous thoughts and feelings. As President Boyd K. Packer explained, "If one becomes critical and harbors negative feelings, the Spirit will withdraw. Only when they repent will the Spirit return. My experience is that the channels of inspiration always follow that order."[66] If we want to be in tune with the Spirit, we must choose daily to be clean and worthy, both in thought and deed.

Our ability to receive revelation may even increase with our chosen level of worthiness and discipleship. As President George Albert Smith taught, "Each of us is entitled to the inspiration of the Lord in proportion to the manner in which we live a godly life."[67] Elder Richard G. Scott stated similarly, "When we receive help from our Father in Heaven, it is in response to faith, obedience, and the proper use of agency."[68] The equation is simple enough: the more we show our obedience and prove our worthiness, the more Heavenly Father will be willing to pour His Spirt out upon us.

If we choose to disobey the commandments that God has given us, to harbor negativity, to make poor choices, or to show through our actions that we have forgotten who we are, then we cannot have the Spirit with us. As King Benjamin taught his people, "And now, I say unto you, my brethren, that after ye have known and have been taught all these things, if ye should transgress and go contrary to that which has been spoken, that ye do withdraw yourselves from the Spirit of the Lord, that it may have no place in you to guide you in wisdom's paths that ye may be blessed, prospered, and preserved" (Mosiah 2:36). Note where the responsibility falls: "ye do withdraw *yourselves*." Personal worthiness is our obligation if we are to keep the gift our Father has given us.

Ask and Ye Shall Receive

We can't expect Heavenly Father to give without us doing anything in return. Once we demonstrate our faith, desire, and worthiness, we must simply ask. No message appears more in the scriptures than "ask and ye shall receive." More than forty times in the scriptures we find some variation of that phrase (for examples, see Matthew 21:22; 1 John 3:22; 1 Nephi 15:11; Enos 1:15; Mosiah 4:21; D&C 4:7; Moses 6:52). We cannot receive unless we have asked. That is a message that our Father in Heaven clearly wanted to get across to His children. As Elder Gerald Lund explains, "Through asking, we exercise our agency and initiate the contact. Surely with more than forty invitations, we may feel completely comfortable in approaching the Father and asking Him for things in prayer. In fact, we have been commanded to do this so often, we should not feel comfortable until we are doing so on a regular basis."[69] God wants us to ask!

What should we say when we come to Him with the desires of our hearts? We can ask to have His Spirit with us, to lead and guide us and show us what He would have us do. Personal revelation often comes as a result of a plea. Indeed, consider the experience of Joseph Smith and the greatest revelation of the latter days. The Restoration of Christ's Church came as a result of a young boy coming to His Father in prayer with a question. Only then did that boy receive a visitation from God the Father and His Son Jesus Christ. Asking opened the door to receiving the answers he sought.

Likewise, when we have questions or are in need of divine guidance, we must ask. The flow of revelation will only happen if we do our part. President Boyd K. Packer, president of the Quorum of the Twelve Apostles, stated clearly how important our end of the channel is:

> You have your agency, and inspiration does not—perhaps cannot— flow unless you ask for it, or someone asks for you. No message in scripture is repeated more often than the invitation, even the command, to pray—to ask. Prayer is so essential a part of revelation that without it the veil may remain closed to you. . . . Prayer is *your* personal key to heaven. The lock is on your side of the veil.[70]

God has given each of us a *personal key* to heaven. How do we unlock the door? How do we pray in a way that will open that sacred channel to our Father in Heaven? Must we memorize particular phrases? Should we feel intimidated by our inadequacies when we realize we are talking to the King and Creator of us all? Should we emulate Enos with his penitent hours on his knees?

Just as we want our own children to come to us with honesty and love and faith in us, all our Father requests is that we talk to Him in faith. I love Elder Richard G. Scott's counsel: "Don't worry about your clumsily expressed feelings. Just talk to your compassionate, understanding Father. You are His precious child whom He loves perfectly and wants to help. As you pray, recognize that Father in Heaven is near and He is listening."[71] What a beautiful promise for each of us, as imperfect as we are.

Elder Scott goes on to explain that sometimes we just need to learn to ask the right questions. He says, "Consider changing from asking for the things you want to honestly seeking what He wants for you. Then as you learn His will, pray that you will be led to have the strength to fulfill it."[72] How often do we pray simply for what we want and forget that our all-knowing Father knows what we need?

President Spencer W. Kimball had similar thoughts about prayer, counseling that perhaps we are so focused on our own limited view that we forget the important phrase "Thy will be done." He suggests that when we consider how we pray to the Father, we should ask ourselves a few important questions:

> Did you say: "Father in Heaven, I love you, I believe in you, I know you are omniscient. I am honest. I am sincerely desirous of doing right. I know you can see the end from the beginning. You can see the future. You can discern if under this situation I present, I will have peace or turmoil, happiness or sorrow, success or failure. Tell me, please, loved Heavenly Father, and I promise to do what you tell me to do." Have you prayed that way? Don't you think it might be wise? Are you courageous enough to pray that prayer?[73]

I remember fifteen years ago when I was seriously dating Scott and deciding if he was the man I was supposed to spend the rest of eternity with. *Deciding* isn't even really the right word. I wanted to marry this guy, I was sure of that. But I knew that before I made the decision final, I needed to get down on my knees. I almost, *almost*, didn't want to. I didn't want any chance that Heavenly Father might say no. Ultimately I made the choice to ask anyway, hoping that the answer would be, "Yes, you are good to go." I needn't have worried because the feeling I got almost immediately upon kneeling was, "You already know." That confirmation filled every step forward with confidence, knowing that my Father in Heaven smiled on us.

We can trust that when we put ourselves in our Father's hands and ask Him for guidance, He will only guide us in ways that will be for our ultimate good. He knows everything from beginning to end. He knows our fears, He knows our shortcomings, He knows our sufferings, and He knows everything about our children and their needs too. He knows what lies on the path ahead and what would be best for those forks in the road. When we humbly allow ourselves to ask for what He sees is right for us, we give ourselves the best opportunity for the greatest happiness.

He wants us to come home to Him. Our joy and success is His whole "work" and "glory" (Moses 1:39). We must simply remember the precious gift we have been given to call upon Him, never taking it for granted. As Elder Richard G. Scott said, "Think of it: the absolute Supreme Being, the most all-knowing, all-seeing, all-powerful personage, encourages you and me, as insignificant as we are, to converse with Him as our Father."[74] Asking for help is our privilege.

Seek and Ye Shall Find

As I mentioned previously, one of the most frequently repeated phrases in the scriptures is "seek and ye shall find." The word *seek* is an active word, suggesting we must do something. We must be actively looking for answers and inspiration if we are to receive them. Beyond listening for our own personal inspiration, we can seek for answers in the scriptures and through the words of prophets, both ancient and modern.

Elder Robert D. Hales summarized his feelings about the power of the scriptures this way: "When we want to speak to God, we pray. And when we want Him to speak to us, we search the scriptures; for His words are spoken through His prophets."[75]

Elder Bruce R. McConkie spent a good portion of his life studying and writing about the scriptures and the restored gospel. Through his study, he discovered what he called "one of the best-kept secrets of the kingdom." That secret is this, as he explained simply: "The scriptures open the door to the receipt of revelation."[76] In the scriptures are the secrets of heaven, which have been experienced, witnessed, and recorded by prophets of God.

Of course, the scriptures aren't going to open anything if they sit gathering dust on our nightstands. Remember, *seeking* implies action. Indeed, the scriptures tell us just how to do that. We read in 2 Nephi that we must "*feast* upon the words of Christ; for behold, the words of Christ will tell you all things what ye should do" (32:3; italics added). I can't say I've had enough scripture study sessions that I would describe as a feast. Mine have often been more of a casual sampling, reading here a little and there a little. *Feasting* implies nourishing a great hunger, poring through the words with intensity and desire. That is how Heavenly Father would have us study—as though we truly recognize the treasure in our hands. When we study that way, we have the power to open the doors of inspiration.

In addition to searching intensely, He also wants us to study these precious books regularly for inspiration. As Christ taught the Nephites, "And now, behold, I say unto you, that ye ought to search these things. Yea, a commandment I give unto you that ye search these things *diligently*." (3 Nephi 23:1; italics added). *Merriam-Webster's* online dictionary defines *diligent* as "characterized by steady, earnest, and energetic effort." Ask yourself, "Can I describe my scripture study that way?" If not, then a little revamp might make the difference between a casual read and the kind of study that opens the windows of heaven.

While the scriptures contain the words of prophets of old, we have other opportunities to study modern-day prophets through general conference addresses and writings in Church magazines. I remember sitting in a graduate school course once when the professor was teaching about post-modernism. She was explaining that this theory suggests we cannot know truth because we are all in the world, and no one has an objective view from outside; everything is subjective. I realized in that moment the great blessing of being directed by a modern-day prophet. We *can* know truth because God, with His perfect, omniscient perspective, communicates with our prophet, who communicates with us. Even as the world around us shifts and changes, our Father in Heaven keeps in contact, regularly updating His liaison on earth with everything we need to know.

We have the opportunity twice a year to listen to the words of inspired prophets and leaders. This is when God can clearly communicate to us through His chosen servants. If we are not able to tune in then, we have the opportunity to read everything as soon as the day after it was spoken. Do we grasp with both hands this chance to be inspired? President Harold B. Lee taught how essential the messages from these conferences are: "How in the world is the Lord going to get over to you what He wants you to do if you are not there when He says it, and you do not take the time to read it after it has been said?"[77] God talks to us through His inspired leaders. We need to tune in if we want to hear what He has to say.

Clearing the Noise

We refer to the Spirit as a "still, small voice." Can we expect to hear and feel something like that if we are constantly surrounded by noise, whether that's music, television, people, or other distractions? We give ourselves the best chance to hear our Father's voice if we can clear the noise and make room for quiet—not all the time, but when we are really ready to listen.

President Boyd K. Packer likened our ability to be spiritually in tune to the channels of communication in a military invasion. He said, "The first order issued by a commander mounting a military invasion is the jamming of the channels of communication of those he intends to conquer. Irreverence suits the purposes of the adversary by obstructing the delicate channels of revelation in both mind and spirit."[78] *Irreverence* here is just one type of noise that keeps us from hearing the Spirit, but that word could be replaced with anything that keeps us from being free to listen. If we want to hear important communications from our Father, then we can't have the channels jammed with distractions.

Ask yourself, "When have I been most in tune with the promptings of the Spirit?" We read in the scriptures that an important way to receive inspiration is to "meditate upon these things; give thyself wholly to them; that thy profiting may appear to all" (1 Timothy 4:15). To meditate upon something suggests more than a quick think through. It suggests quiet pondering and time devoted to reflection. As we read in Alma, one way to do this is to "pour out your souls in your closets, and your secret places, and in your wilderness" (34:26).

As a busy mom, I'm not always good at escaping to my wilderness. Often from the time I get up to the time I go to sleep, I haven't had a minute of quiet time to ponder and listen. Whether it's getting kids out the door for school, reading the headlines, going to the store, folding laundry, getting to soccer practice, making dinner, helping with homework or piano, or thinking through what needs to happen tomorrow, I am just busy! Sometimes when I finally get in bed, I just want to say a quick prayer and pass out without ever really listening for a return message. If I want to have a few minutes to clear the noise, I have to make that happen somewhere in the day when I can be open to inspiration.

I think many moms feel the same way. Carving out a moment of peace takes some conscious effort, but it is so worth it for the perspective and inspiration it can bring. When I think about it and make the effort to clear the noise, I will turn off the music in the car for a few minutes or just have quiet in the house while I fold laundry, or I might even do some pondering while I mow the lawn. My friend Stacey finds her quiet moment in the morning. She said, "I think it is extremely important to take time to communicate with and listen to the Lord. My most sacred time is when I am getting ready, uninterrupted, in the morning. This rarely happens, but this is usually when I receive the answers to any questions I am worried about."

Another friend has a quiet bench where she can retreat when the chaos of a household of eight gets to be too much. It was particularly useful when her children were young and all living at home. She said, "Inspiration I know is something I've tried to be sensitive to. There is so much living in the house. It's hard when I have a child who wants to play music or watch TV all the time. I need quiet time. I have a little red bench outside. I love my bench. I'd go out there, and no one would discover me for fifteen or twenty minutes. It was a time to have a moment to think—a place to retreat, even though I was still home and still available."

President Henry B. Eyring has testified about the importance of quiet and peace for his own experiences receiving revelation. After one particular experience hearing the whisperings of the Spirit during a time of decision making, he came to this realization: "I learned from that experience and countless repetitions that the description of the Holy Ghost as a still, small voice is real. It is poetic, but it is not poetry. Only when my heart has been still and quiet, in submission like a little child, has the Spirit been clearly audible to my heart and mind."[79] We too can catch those whisperings if we have turned down the noise of the world enough to hear.

The Power of Fasting

Fasting can be another way to boost our sensitivity to revelation, putting our body in a submissive state so we can be more open to the things of the Spirit. Alma had a great desire to know the truthfulness of the gospel. After preparing himself through fasting and prayer, he received a witness. He writes, "Behold, I say unto you they are made known unto me by the Holy Spirit of God. Behold, I have fasted and prayed many days that I might know these things of myself. And now I do know of myself that they are true; for the Lord God hath made them manifest unto me by his Holy Spirit; and this is the spirit of revelation which is

Heidi Poelman

in me" (Alma 5:46). Note how Alma directly connects the spirit of revelation with his preparation of prayer and fasting.

We learn later in the book of Alma that the sons of Mosiah had a similar experience in which they "had given themselves to much prayer, and fasting; *therefore* they had the spirit of prophecy, and the spirit of revelation" (Alma 17:3; italics added). The scriptures state clearly that these young missionaries had the spirit of revelation because of their prayer and fasting.

As mothers, we have the opportunity to turn to fasting as well when we are in particular need of spiritual guidance. One neighbor shared with me her experience fasting to know if the man she was dating was the man she should marry, the man who could be the future father of her children. She was actually already on track for a wedding, with her ring and dress, when she decided she needed to fast to know for sure. It took two and a half days of fasting before she felt she finally had a firm answer.

The answer she received was no, along with a thought that popped into her mind. She suddenly realized that, as she said, "I needed to marry someone better than I was, who would help me be stronger." That thought helped her realize this man would not help her be stronger in life. When she came to her own mother to share her experience, she learned that her mother had experienced similar promptings that the marriage wasn't right. That's when this young and courageous woman knew for sure she had her answer, one that she describes as "the hardest answer I ever got." Still, looking back she knows she made the right choice. As she explained, "I know for a fact now that I shouldn't have married him because of what he did with his life after we were together."

I admire this woman for her desire to do what was right by putting her life in the hands of her Father in Heaven with intense fasting and prayer. Who knows where her life might have gone had she not decided to fast until she knew for sure what she was supposed to do. Happily, she later found the man she was supposed to marry. Together they have five children and are strong members of the Church.

We are promised in the scriptures that if we are willing to yield to our Father's will and show our faith in Him with fasting and prayer, then we can have His presence with us. As President Harold B. Lee counseled, "The Lord said to Isaiah, that those who would thus fast and deal out their bread to the hungry, could call and the Lord would answer, could cry and the Lord would say, 'Here I am.'"[80] What a beautiful promise. If we choose to show our devotion to God through fasting, then He will answer our call.

Write It Down

Part of the blessing of receiving personal revelation as mothers is actually using that divine counsel to bless our families. How many times have you had an inclination to do something or say something and then not acted on it or simply forgotten about it? One key to receiving more revelation is acting on the revelation we receive. We can't act on something if we have forgotten what it was. Writing down promptings is one way to make sure we remember to act.

Elder Richard G. Scott shared his sacred experience recording revelation while visiting a Spanish branch in Mexico City. While he was listening to a speaker, he started having spiritual impressions about his role and how he could be a better instrument in the Lord's hands. He said, "As each impression came, I carefully wrote it down. In the process, I was given precious truths that I greatly needed in order to be a more effective servant of the Lord. . . . I was given specific directions, instructions, and conditioned promises that have beneficially altered the course of my life."[81]

Later, during Sunday School, impressions started flowing again, so Elder Scott "continued to write the feelings that flooded into my mind and heart as faithfully as possible." After praying to ask if there was anything more he needed to know, this experience of receiving and recording revelation happened twice more later that morning. The last impressions he received he describes as "some of the most precious, specific, personal direction one could hope to obtain in this life." Elder Scott is confident that taking the time to write down his promptings is what blessed him with more. Specifically, he said, "Had I not responded to the first impressions and recorded them, I would not have received the last, most precious guidance."[82]

Recording our promptings is a way to acknowledge, study, and remember the sacred messages our Father sends to us. My mother-in-law, Kerry, has a knack for this. While she was raising her children, she made sure to pay special attention to promptings and always have a way to record them nearby. She said, "I would always write things down when they came to me. I would have thoughts like, 'Ask Danny about this,' or, 'I need to have some one-on-one time with Scott.' I kept a pen and paper by my bed and in the bathroom. I didn't want to miss a prompting."

I have found of my own experiences with promptings that when I write them down, they become more precious to me, and I can look back and recognize the Father's hand in my life. Finding ways to pay attention to, record, and remember our spiritual experiences will bless us as we seek guidance and strength as mothers.

A Humble Heart

Part of being open to revelation from the Spirit is having the humility to know we can't figure out everything on our own. Just like as parents we hope our children will be open to our guidance and teaching, Heavenly Father wants us to be willing to seek His counsel.

We are told in the scriptures how important humility is when it comes to receiving instruction from above. The Lord gave a revelation to Joseph Smith about the people living in the last days, where He promised that "inasmuch as they were *humble* they might be made strong, and blessed from on high, and receive knowledge from time to time" (D&C 1:28; italics added). Later in the Doctrine and Covenants we find this equation: "Be thou *humble*; and the Lord thy God shall lead thee by the hand, and give thee answer to thy prayers" (D&C 112:10; italics added). The

Lord also instructed Brigham Young about the way to access the Spirit, saying, "Let him that is ignorant learn wisdom by *humbling* himself and calling upon the Lord his God, that his eyes may be opened that he may see, and his ears opened that he may hear; for my Spirit is sent forth into the world to enlighten the *humble* and contrite (D&C 136:32–33; italics added).

We can be blessed from on high. We can receive knowledge. We can be in tune with the Spirit. And we can receive the answers we seek. These are beautiful and powerful promises based on a simple prerequisite: humility.

Kerry, has a strong testimony of the need for humility in order to receive personal revelation for her family. As she explained, "I tried to always have a repentant heart and be open to receiving instruction. I had to shut off the pride." Her words rang true to me as I thought about the difference between constantly relying on our own abilities and listening for instruction from the One who knows infinitely more than we do. As Elder Richard G. Scott so beautifully described:

> Humility is that quality that permits us to be taught from on high through the Spirit or to be taught from sources whose origin was inspiration from the Lord, such as the scriptures and the comments of the prophets. Humility is the precious, fertile soil of righteous character. In it the seeds of personal growth germinate. When cultivated through the exercise of faith, pruned by repentance, and fortified by obedience and good works, such seeds produce the cherished fruit of spiritual direction.[83]

Pride ruins the soil and stunts our ability to grow. We can't be open to receiving direction if we think we have everything figured out already. Humility is that quality that allows us to be open to ideas that are better than our own. As a mother, I constantly find myself in situations where I have no idea what I'm doing. My children are growing and changing every day, and they are unique in how they learn and respond to the world. I know full well that I don't have all the answers. I also know that my Father in Heaven does. The more I am able to lower my pride and remember humility, the more I am open to receiving answers from above that can bless my family.

In His House

Can we possibly get any closer to our Father in Heaven than in His own house? He has promised us clearly that when we visit the temple, "My presence shall be there, for I will come into it" (D&C 97:16). President Ezra Taft Benson described how important visiting the temple has been to his own experience with personal revelation. He said,

> In the peace of these lovely temples, sometimes we find solutions to the serious problems of life. Under the influence of the Spirit, sometimes pure knowledge flows to us there. Temples are places of personal revelation. When I have been weighed down by a problem or a difficulty, I have gone to the house of the Lord with a prayer in my heart for answers. These answers have come in clear and unmistakable ways.[84]

Visiting the temple regularly is another powerful way to strengthen our ability to receive personal revelation when we are in need of guidance from our Divine Parent. One mother, Carla, shared how she was able to be more in tune with guidance from Heavenly Father during a particular phase of her life when she had the opportunity to visit the temple frequently:

> While I was raising our kids, there was a time when I ended up being at the temple for four weeks in a row for different reasons. I was so overwhelmed with how many ideas came into my head with parenting. I sat and started writing them down on a piece of paper, and I filled the front and back with ideas that had come. I was blown away by everything that had come to me. I could not believe He told me all that in four weeks.

Hearing about that kind of experience makes me want to visit the temple more often! It seems the veil simply becomes a bit thinner when we are pondering within the walls of His sacred space. I had an experience recently in the temple where I had prayed for any inspiration He wanted to send me as a mother. While I was sitting through an endowment session, I had some quiet time to reflect and listen. My thoughts wandered to what my children would be like when they are grown—something I don't often think about. I imagined my son as a missionary: confident, happy, handsome, and eager to serve. I imagined my daughters getting ready for college: beautiful, excited, and full of ideas for their futures. I don't know why those thoughts crept into my head, but I enjoyed thinking about what they might become some day, about their wonderful potential as spirits of an eternal God. The experience caused me to come home and look at each of them, small and asleep in their beds, and thank Heavenly Father for letting me help them through their mortal journey of discovery and growth.

Feeling especially in tune while we are in the temple is a blessing that motivates me to return as often as I can. What's great is that the spiritual boost from inside the temple gates seems to linger even after we leave. Many of the women I interviewed testified that they felt closer to the Spirit for some time after they left the temple as well. One friend of mine described it this way:

> I definitely notice that when I regularly attend the temple, I am more in tune in significant ways. It is in these times that I feel almost a minute-by-minute spiritual guidance in things like how to spend my time and what to focus on. Oftentimes, I find myself reading just the right scripture to answer a family problem, picking up the right book that gives me the best solution, or getting an inspired phone call from a friend who has just the right advice.

Another mother, Julie, agreed that her experiences at the temple not only bless her with guidance while she is there but also strengthen the Spirit in her home after she leaves. As she said,

> I am much more in tune to the promptings of the Spirit when I attend the temple. When I need guidance or just a bit of peace and comfort, I go to the temple. With a traveling husband, it is so difficult to find a time to go, but my body and spirit truly ache to go regularly. I rarely get a quiet moment with four children running around. In the temple, I can ponder and pray. I feel the Lord

blesses me even after and gives me added strength and inspiration that following week. It seems to wear off quickly though, so my need to go back returns rather quickly too.

If we are looking for a way to strengthen our ability to be in tune with our Father in Heaven, we need look no further than the sacred walls of the temple. Inside, we can receive peace and inspiration that will affect us not only there but in our homes as well. President Ezra Taft Benson put it plainly when he said, "I promise you that, with increased attendance in the temples of our God, you shall receive increased personal revelation to bless your life."[85] To me, that's a promise worth acting on as often as I can.

Using Our Own Resources

Sometimes my kids start asking me to do things for them that I know they can do for themselves—things like, "Will you get me a drink? Will you clean up my toys? Will you cut up my pancake?" It's easier to have someone do it for you, right? My response is simple: "If you can do it by yourself, go ahead. If you've tried your best and still need help, I'll be here." I think God operates in much the same way.

Yes, He wants us to come to Him for help, but He also expects us to do everything in our power to make good choices and move along in life as best as we can. When we need extra comfort or guidance, He is there for us. We should not expect Him to make important decisions for us or tell us what to do every step of the way. Life is a test, remember? He has given us tools and resources to make our own way much of the time. We shouldn't rely on Him for things we are actually quite capable of. For example, Elder Dallin H. Oaks tells a story of a woman who bore her testimony about how her husband even prayed in the shopping aisle to know which brand of canned vegetables to buy. A bit much? That's what Elder Oaks thought. He said, "The Spirit is not likely to give us revelations on matters that are trivial. . . . I believe the Lord expects us to make most of our decisions by using the intelligence and experience He has given us."[86]

I recently had a mothering experience where I came to appreciate God's desire for us to rely on our own resources. I was having a day when I was struggling with a particular child's attitude. I felt a bit overwhelmed by the end of the day and prayed to Heavenly Father that I would know how to help this child be strong and joyful. I listened and thought the matter over in my mind, but I didn't feel any particular answer or comfort in that moment. The next day, however, I pulled out a favorite parenting book by an expert in positive psychology and looked up chapters that related to what I was dealing with at home. After reading those chapters, I felt renewed strength as I found relevant answers. The Spirit seemed to be reassuring me that I had done the right thing: prayed for strength from above while also getting to work with the resources at my fingertips.

Heavenly Father wants us to use what He has given us. We see evidence of His feelings on the matter in the Doctrine and Covenants after Oliver Cowdery came to Harmony, Pennsylvania, in 1829 and began acting as scribe for the Prophet Joseph Smith. Oliver desired the gift of translation, which the Lord was willing to grant, but Oliver failed in his attempt. Why? This is the explanation Oliver received: "Behold, you have not understood; you have supposed that I would give it unto you, when *you took no thought save it was to ask me.* But, behold, I say unto you, that you must study it out in your mind; then you must ask me if it be right, and if it is right I will cause that your bosom shall burn within you; therefore, you shall feel that it is right" (D&C 9:7–8; italics added). Heavenly Father wanted Oliver to do more than just ask. He wanted him to seek, to study, and to give it his best effort first.

The same requirement applies to us. Elder Boyd K. Packer said it well:

> We are expected to use the light and knowledge we already possess to work out our lives. We should not need a revelation to instruct us to be up and about our duty, for we have been told to

do that already in the scriptures; nor should we expect revelation to replace the spiritual or temporal intelligence which we have already received—only to extend it. We must go about our life in an ordinary, workaday way, following the routines and rules and regulations that govern life.[87]

In other words, we should not expect constant revelation when we have already been given such wonderful direction about how to go about our lives. We must simply keep doing what we know is best based on the knowledge and guidelines Heavenly Father has already laid out for us. As we go, we can continually pray for any additional revelation He sees fit to send. The point is, don't sit around waiting for Him to tell you what to do. As President Gordon B. Hinckley said, "I don't know how to get anything done except getting on my knees and pleading for help and then getting on my feet and going to work."[88]

Indeed, much of the seeking and listening for answers occurs after we have prayed and then gone to work. Elder Gerald Lund put it this way: "Obtaining revelation is not a passive experience. We don't just toss off a prayer, then sit back and wait for the answer to come. We must choose to actively participate in the revelatory process. Asking is how the process begins, but it is not how it ends."[89]

God wants us to think, to figure things out, and to work out our questions using to the best of our ability all the resources, gifts, and inspiration He has already given us. Once we have done that, He welcomes us to come to Him for help. He wants us to pray for direction and guidance. He doesn't want us to stop there. After we have thought it out, tried our best, and prayed for guidance, then we can get back to work while we wait for His instruction.

Practice Listening

Elder Boyd K. Packer once shared a story about a naturalist named John Burroughs. One summer evening, John was taking a walk through a crowded city park. He noticed the beautiful song of a bird above the noise of the city. He stopped and listened, and then he looked around and noticed that no one else had heard the song. He decided to do a test. He took a coin from his pocket, flipped it in the air, and let it hit the pavement. The coin struck the pavement with a sound that was no louder than the song of the bird. That sound the people noticed. Why did they notice the coin but not the bird? Perhaps because they were not used to the song of a bird, but money plays an ongoing and important role in most people's lives. Elder Packer compared our ability to hear the beautiful song of the bird to listening for the Holy Ghost. He said, "It is difficult to separate from all the sounds of city traffic the song of a bird. But you can hear it. You can hear it plainly if you train yourself to listen for it."[90] Likewise, the ability to notice the whisperings of the Spirit comes only with practice.

When I first became a new mother, I worried about my ability to hear my baby's hunger cries in the middle of the night. I've always been a deep sleeper, and not much wakes me. But after we brought this tiny infant home, I realized that my mother's ears became easily in tune with his whimpers. No matter what time of night, I woke to the slightest sounds from the crib, alerting me that my little one needed something. With practice, that became easier and easier. He did not have to work hard to reach me because my ears were ready and waiting to hear him. Are our ears likewise constantly ready to hear communication from our Father in Heaven? Have we practiced enough to know what His voice sounds and feels like?

Listening is the second half of prayer. Too often we focus so much on the asking part that we forget entirely about what comes next. As President Hinckley once described, "The trouble with most of our prayers is that we give them as if we were picking up the phone and ordering groceries—we place our order and hang up."[91]

As a busy mother, I know that sometimes it's hard to find quiet moments to listen during the day. Our home is often full of life and activity with our children and their projects and friends. When I'm not at home, I'm usually driving people from one thing to the next, trying to juggle school, music, scouts, and sports. But if I'm thinking about it, and if I choose to make it happen, I can find those nuggets of quiet time when I can listen. That might be in the morning before kids wake up, the short windows while my two oldest are at school and my youngest is at preschool, in the car after I've dropped everyone off where they need to be, or late at night when kids are tucked in their beds. The quiet moments are there—I just need to be careful not to fill those moments with more noise of life (which I am often tempted to do with music, a fun television show, or an audio book). Turning off the noise so we can really be in tune to our Father's voice is essential. Elder Richard G. Scott summarized his view of the importance of finding a quiet time to listen:

> He will always hear your prayers and will invariably answer them. However, His answers will seldom come while you are on your knees praying, even when you may plead for an immediate response. Rather, He will prompt you in quiet moments when the Spirit can most effectively touch your mind and heart. Hence, you should find periods of quiet time to recognize when you are being instructed and strengthened. His pattern causes you to grow.[92]

Elder Packer once compared the experience of listening through the noise of the world for the Spirit to his experience as a World War II pilot flying through a storm. Before the high-tech electronic equipment of our day, pilots had to listen for a radio beam that would direct them as to whether or not they were on course. If the pilot flew too far to one side of the steady signal, he would hear a "dit-da" sound. If he flew too far to the other side, the signal would change to "da-dit." When flying through the inevitable storms that came from time to time, a pilot would have to listen through static and interference for those slight cues that told him he was on course.

As Elder Packer explained, "The life of many a pilot has depended on his hearing, above the roar of the engines and through all the static and interference, that sometimes weak signal from a distant airfield." He went on to say how we too must listen through the static for our own life-saving signal. "There is a spiritual beam, with a constant signal," he said. "If you know how to pray and how to listen, spiritually listen, you may move through life, through clear weather, through storms, through wars, through peace, and be all right."[93]

As mothers, if we want to be in tune to hear our Father's voice above the fray, we need to give Him an opportunity to reach us. That doesn't mean we will hear Him every time we turn off the noise. But if He has something He needs to tell us, we probably won't hear it unless we have created moments when we can listen.

Pray Always

Heavenly Father doesn't want us to only cry out to Him when we are in need of something. As President Howard W. Hunter said, "If prayer is only a spasmodic cry at the time of crisis, then it is utterly selfish, and we come to think of God as a repairman or a service agency to help us only in our emergencies. We should remember the Most High day and night—always—not only at times when all other assistance has failed and we desperately need help."[94] We must commit to pray always, that we may always have His Spirit to guide, direct, and comfort us. He wants us to develop a relationship, a pattern of prayer that is consistent, diligent, personal, and sincere. He is not just the deliverer of goods and the solver of all our earthly problems. He is our Father, who knows us, knows our needs, and wants to guide us along, especially as we raise and teach our children. Creating and maintaining that relationship requires more than a shout out before we hit the pillow at night.

I think as mothers it's easy for us to relate to the feeling that sometimes children reach out only when they need something. So many times I am the person my kids come to when they want something—a drink, some breakfast, a ride, help with a bow or a button, or someone to take a handful of trash. While I am grateful to be that person who can help my children, how I love it when they reach out for something more meaningful, whether it's telling me about their day, thanking me for the dinner I made, saying "I love you," or simply asking me what I think about something. Those are the rewarding moments that help me feel really connected to my kids. I imagine Heavenly Father feels the same way when we choose to reach out to Him in love and gratitude. The more we do that, the stronger our relationship becomes.

Kerry described that process as a constant dialogue. "I felt like I had to be constantly praying," she said. "I was always searching and pondering. That takes time. I have to listen. It was a dialogue all the time." That dialogue showed up in different ways throughout the day, whether it was asking why a child might be upset or wondering how to solve a particular problem. She was always asking for guidance and then listening for a response. Sometimes, she said, she would just stop and stare at the wall for a few minutes to find peace and listen. "That was often when I would receive a quickening of the mind," she said. "I'd get goose bumps all the time."

Heavenly Father has been quite clear with us about His feelings on prayer and what is in store for us if we follow His counsel: "Pray *always*, and I will pour out my Spirit upon you, and great shall be your blessing—yea, even more than if you should obtain treasures of earth" (D&C 19:38; italics added). Prayer is what opens the channel of communication. Our Father wants to guide us. We just need to be constantly open to the messages He is willing and ready to send.

Chapter 11

When the Heavens Seem Silent

Relying on Faith, Trust, and Patience

SOMETIMES DESPITE all our best efforts to be worthy and prayerful and to listen for our Father's voice, we hear nothing but a deafening silence. We feel as though we have been forgotten. Of course, deep down, we know who we are and *whose* we are. We know we haven't been left alone and that our Creator could never forget a child He loves. Then why does Heavenly Father sometimes seem to not answer our prayers?

I remember sitting at a recent Time Out for Women event in Salt Lake City where I listened to Broadway singer Sandra Turley tell her story of trying to bring children into her family. After years of trying to get pregnant on their own, Sandra and her husband opted to try in vitro fertilization—an expensive fertility treatment. While Sandra was waiting for the procedure, her husband gave her a priesthood blessing in which he was inspired to say that in the next nine months they would have a baby in their arms. Sandra, ecstatic, thought their prayers were being answered.

Shortly after the procedure, Sandra found out she was pregnant. But not long after that, she miscarried the baby and was left again with painfully empty arms. Neither husband nor wife could understand why the blessing she received had said they would have a baby when this was the outcome. Then a seemingly miraculous phone call came. Sandra and her husband were being offered the chance to adopt a baby girl that was going to be born right around the same time their own baby would have come. After much thought and prayer, they decided they would love nothing more than the opportunity to adopt this baby girl. Again, they thought their prayers had been answered.

Months of busy and excited preparation went by, and the little girl was born. Sandra and her husband flew to New York to meet the baby and bring her home. They loved this baby deeply and immediately. They took care of her for four weeks and then got another life-altering phone call. In the state of New York, a birth mother has thirty days to change her mind about an adoption. The birth mother of this baby girl, within her rights, wanted her baby back. Devastated, Sandra and her husband had no choice.

I can't imagine the feelings of hopelessness and confusion this couple experienced. Surely they had to be asking, "Why?" They were living good lives and had the potential to be amazing parents. God knew that, didn't He? They had been prayerful and had even experienced a priesthood blessing with the promise of children. I can imagine their cries to their Father in Heaven as something similar to Joseph Smith when he was suffering in Liberty Jail, asking "O God, where art thou? And where is the pavilion that covereth thy hiding place? How long shall thy hand be stayed?" (D&C 121:1–2).

They didn't know. But in that painful hour, after their years of trying to conceive, after the loss of the baby they finally did conceive, and after the loss of the baby they had adopted, surely this couple was asking why the heavens seemed to be so silent.

The answer Joseph Smith received to his cry was this: "All these things shall give thee experience, and shall be for thy good" (D&C 122:7). We don't know why we are asked to suffer sometimes, and we don't always know why our prayers are not answered right away or are not answered in the way we hope they will be. We don't know why Joseph was left to suffer in jail, or why Sandra and her husband experienced what they did, or why good people have to endure hard trials. As Elder Gerald Lund explained, "We can't answer those questions except to say that the Lord determines all aspects of personal revelation, including the intensity and duration of tutorial experiences."[95]

The timing of answers to prayer are not up to us to decide, but instead they are left up to a loving, all-powerful Father, who knows far more than we do about our circumstances and our future. In the case of Sandra Turley, shortly after she was asked to give her adopted baby girl back to the birth mother, she found out she was pregnant. In the seven years after, she and her husband were able to have four children on their own—a blessing they couldn't possibly have imagined. The Lord knew all along what would become of this young family.

Why does God have us wait sometimes? Why does He ask us to be patient and sometimes even suffer? Why does He not always grant us the desires of our hearts? I love what author and Holocaust survivor Corrie ten Boom has written on the subject. She says, "Every experience God gives us, every person He puts in our lives is the perfect preparation for a future that only He can see."[96] This chapter will explore a few of the reasons why a loving Father allows the heavens to occasionally fall silent while we are tested and tried.

When the Wait Is for Our Good

One of my heroes is Helen Keller, who lived from the time she was very young without the ability to see or hear. I can't imagine living that way, and I certainly can't imagine doing it happily. To me, Helen is the epitome of strength and perseverance through struggle. She lived an extraordinary life. She once described what she thought built character in an individual, and I can't think of anyone who would know better. She attributed to having said, "Character cannot be developed in ease and quiet. Only through the experience of trial and suffering can the soul be strengthened, ambition inspired, and success achieved." And so it is with us. When sometimes we think God has left us alone, He is really only allowing us to be strengthened. There is a reason.

We are all tried in different ways depending on what we, personally, need to experience to grow. Relief Society General President Linda Burton speaks of some of her children needing to wait patiently for years as they were trying to find their eternal companions. Probably at times the experience was frustrating and difficult as these young adults wondered how in the world they were supposed to start their families and do what God wanted if they couldn't find the right partner. As Sister Burton put it, "At times the heavens even seemed closed to them as they prayed. When the Lord's timing conflicts with our own desires, trust that there might be some preparatory experiences the Lord needs us to have before our prayers are answered."[97]

Occasionally, Heavenly Father waits to answer our prayers because something needs to happen in our life that we just can't see yet. My friend Jen experienced a waiting period in her life that felt to her as though God was not answering her prayers. But there was a reason. After having her second child, Jen was having a hard time getting pregnant again. Months went by without success. She felt frustrated, disappointed, and confused because getting pregnant the first two times had been so simple. "I was scared that I might not be able to have any more children," she said. She prayed and even received priesthood blessings with no result. It didn't seem fair. "Why couldn't I have this righteous desire of my heart?" she wondered.

While Jen was going through this waiting period, she noticed unusual bumps on her cheek that she brushed off as acne, but they wouldn't go away. She finally decided to go to a dermatologist, who told her the bumps were precancerous and that she needed to get them treated immediately. She had to use a painful, aggressive cream on her cheeks for a few months to wipe away the cancer cells. Through the process, she realized why God may have been waiting to answer her prayer for another child: "My doctor told me that it was a good thing I wasn't pregnant, because you can't use this treatment if you are," she said. "Wow! It turned out to be a blessing that I wasn't pregnant, because I was able to take care of a threatening health situation. Luckily, after my treatment, I was able to have the two more children we always wanted."

Jen's story is a powerful reminder to me that our Heavenly Father *always* knows more than we do about whatever situation we are in. It is hard to be patient, especially when the desire of our heart is a righteous one. Sometimes Heavenly Father is just waiting because of an issue we cannot see.

The wait we are asked to endure sometimes simply allows us to develop the faith and perseverance we need to become spiritually strong. We might even consider being grateful for the delay, as frustrating as it may be. As Elder Richard G. Scott said, "Be thankful that sometimes God lets you struggle for a long time before that answer comes. Your character will grow; your faith will increase. There is a relationship between those two: the greater your faith, the stronger your character; and increased character enhances your ability to exercise even greater faith."[98]

Struggle helps us to grow, and this life, after all, is about growth and learning to become more like God. Through the wait, we learn faith. Elder Dallin H. Oaks once put it this way: "Our life's purpose to obtain experience and to develop faith would be frustrated if our Heavenly Father enlightened us immediately on every question or directed us in every act. We must reach conclusions and make decisions and experience the consequences in order to develop self-reliance and faith."[99]

Like the little child whose parent gives in to every demand, if our Father in Heaven answered every prayer just the way we wanted, right when we asked, we could not learn to fight through our hardships. We could not learn patience, fortitude, courage, or how to hear the quiet and subtle whisperings of the still, small voice. As Elder Richard G. Scott surmised, "Were you to receive inspired guidance just for the asking, you would become weak and ever more dependent on Them. They know that essential personal growth will come as you struggle to learn how to be led by the Spirit."[100]

The wait is sometimes what allows each of us to become the person He knows we have the potential to be. We just don't always see clearly why He would make us wait. But if He is holding back, there is always a reason. I like how Elder Dieter F. Uchtdorf summed it up recently during women's conference, making many in attendance chuckle: "I think God knows something we don't."[101]

According to His Time

Sometimes what feels like an outrageously long time to us is, to His divine eyes, just a brief moment. I can relate to the strange relativity of time as a parent. Have you ever noticed how sometimes five minutes to a child feels like an eternity? The other night, my son demonstrated his unique perspective on time when we were at an extended family birthday dinner. I can't remember how the subject came up, but we started talking about how the night before, our printer had broken. That, for me, was the veritable last straw in a string of broken household items. The microwave, the router, the car tires, the garage door, and the furnace already needed repair. When the printer wouldn't work, being tired and pregnant, I broke down in tears. I was probably in that state for five minutes (okay, maybe ten—split between realizing the printer wasn't working and two hours later of trying unsuccessfully with my husband to make it work). At the family dinner the next day, Zach said, "Mom, you were crying for like an hour last night." Everyone laughed while I tried to explain that an hour is not the same thing as a five-minute meltdown. But to my son, it felt like forever.

I imagine that's how Heavenly Father feels sometimes. We, in our impatient and limited mortal perspective, sometimes feel like answers are taking an eternity to come. He, in His divine wisdom, can see such a vastly different view. To Him, even years might feel like only minutes. He must smile sometimes at how impatient His children can be while they wait for His blessing. He has revealed to us, through scripture, how personal revelation will come—not according to our timetable, but according to His: "Therefore, sanctify yourselves that your minds become single to God, and the days will come that you shall see him; for he will unveil his face unto you, and it shall be in *his own time*, and in *his own way*, and according to *his own will*" (D&C 88:68; italics added). Not in our time or in our way or according to our will.

Elder Dallin H. Oaks expanded on the idea of God's time. He said, "Many people do not understand this principle. They believe that when they are ready and when it suits their convenience, they can call upon the Lord and He will immediately respond, even in the precise way they have prescribed. Revelation does not come that way. . . . We cannot force spiritual things."[102] Sometimes, when the heavens seem silent, it is helpful to remember that answers will come according to His will, when He is ready to give them. We can always remember that His goal is to help us reach our eternal potential and to help us find joy in this life and the next. Here is His promise to us: "And they shall also be crowned with blessings from above, yea, and with commandments not a few, and with revelations in their time—they that are faithful and diligent before me" (D&C 59:4). In other words, persist in faith, and blessings will come.

He Wants Us to Act

Sometimes Heavenly Father is waiting on us to act before He will either confirm our decision or let us know we're on the wrong path. Remember the words from the revelation given to Oliver Cowdery when he expected easy guidance: "You have supposed that I would give it unto you, when you took no thought save it was to ask me. But, behold, I say unto you, that you must study it out in your mind; then you must ask me if it be right, and if it is right I will cause that your bosom shall burn within you; therefore, you shall feel that it is right" (D&C 9:7–8).

Heidi Poelman

Scott's grandfather's wife, Annie, had an interesting experience with her decision to get married. A respected doctor who had recently joined the Church, Annie remained single for quite some time. She was well into her thirties and feeling impatient to finally start a family. Several potential suitors had come along, but none really seemed to fit. Finally, one desirable enough widower asked Annie to be his wife. She went to the temple in prayer and sat in the celestial room waiting. *Well?* she thought, expecting God to make the decision for her. Then she recalled the revelation given to Oliver Cowdery in the Doctrine and Covenants and realized that Heavenly Father was waiting on her to make a choice. Then He would either confirm the choice or let her know otherwise.

Annie finally made her decision. "Well, I've made up my mind," she writes in her book *The Simeon Solution*. "I'm going to do it." What happened next surprised her: "The ensuing reply was a single firm but powerful mental '*No!*' The impression was so strong it almost seemed auditory. Startled at the strength of the unexpected answer, I looked up and said out loud, '*What?*'" Still thinking that the strong impression was just her imagination, she went home intending to accept the proposal, ignoring her nagging doubts. Then, as though God realized He hadn't quite gotten through, He sent another message.

Annie was at home the next day when a member of her ward stopped by. He explained that he had the oddest thing happen the night before when he couldn't sleep. He said he had received an impression that Annie was facing a critical decision in her life and that, whatever it was, she was supposed to say no.[103]

Annie was stunned. How could this man have known? She finally resigned herself to the idea that God was sending her a clear message: this was not the right man for her. Only years later did she find out why, when she met Scott's grandfather, a recent widower named Elder Ronald E. Poelman. She quickly came to realize that this was the man she was supposed to marry and build her life with. After they married, Annie and Ron traveled for her medical lectures, and the couple had many opportunities to share the gospel with prominent figures around the globe and share a happy life together. That outcome, it seems, was God's intention. He wasn't going to let her go too far down the wrong road without stopping her in her tracks.

Heavenly Father was willing to guide Annie along in her personal journey. But He wasn't going to give her all the information she wanted to know simply because she asked for it. Instead, He waited for her to make a choice, and then He let her know, unmistakably, that she needed to change course. If it feels like Heavenly Father is not answering a prayer, He may simply be waiting for us to act. He won't let us go too far on the wrong path without a warning that something better lies in another direction.

When the Answer is "Not Yet"

Sometimes what feels like "no" is simply "not yet." When Scott started praying about marrying me, he didn't receive that resounding, confidence-building burning of the bosom right at first. Instead, he felt doubt and confusion as he thought about the idea of getting married. Thinking the answer was no, he called me from London to break up. Only after a few weeks of soul searching alone through Europe did he realize that what he thought was no was really just "not yet." Before he could be a confident husband, first he had to break through his own fears about marriage that stemmed from his parents' divorce. Once he had done that, he received the yes he was looking for.

A similar thing happened to my friend Angelica, who shared her experience with a "not yet" answer in the *Ensign*. She was a young member of the Church living in Sweden and was praying to know whether she should go to BYU. With her goal of a temple marriage, she figured that path made sense. But no matter how hard she prayed for Heavenly Father to bless the decision to go, "It never felt right," she said.

Angelica ultimately decided to scrap her original plans and apply to a university in Sweden instead. Around the same time that she would have left for BYU, she met and fell in love with a recently returned missionary named Jonas. Not long after, Angelica and Jonas were sealed in the temple. They later attended BYU together, graduating on the same day. "Now I look back and see why Heavenly Father initially said no—or really, 'not yet'—to my fervent prayer about attending BYU," Angelica said. "Although He said no to my desire at that particular time, He was actually saying yes to a much more important desire."[104] If Angelica hadn't listened to her initial feelings that she needed to stay in Sweden, she may have never met the man Heavenly Father knew she was supposed to marry.

If we feel like we aren't getting answers to our prayers, or if we feel like Heavenly Father is giving a "no" signal, even to a righteous desire, the answer may really just be "not yet." The only way to know is to follow the promptings of the Spirit and wait to see what Heavenly Father has in store.

He Trusts Us, and We Must Trust Him

Sometimes Heavenly Father doesn't respond simply because He trusts us to make our own decision, following the instruction that He has already given. In return, He expects us to trust Him. Elder Richard G. Scott has said, "This life is an experience in profound trust. . . . To exercise faith is to trust that the Lord knows what He is doing with you and that He can accomplish it for your eternal good even though you cannot understand how He can possibly do it."[105] Elder Scott added to his counsel with what we can do when we feel we are receiving no answer: "You may want to express thanks when that occurs, for it is an evidence of [Heavenly Father's] trust. When you are living worthily and your choice is consistent with the Savior's teachings and you need to act, proceed with trust."[106]

After you have proceeded with your decision, Elder Scott promised that either you will experience a stupor of thought, suggesting you have made a wrong choice, or the decision will be confirmed with a feeling from the Spirit. Either way, he says,

"God will not let you proceed too far without a warning impression if you have made the wrong decision."[107]

As mothers, we have many decisions to make as we try to help our children learn, grow, and become their best selves. I find comfort in knowing that if I am trying my best and using my own knowledge and resources to make a good decision, and I don't feel that I am being led one way or another, it is a sign that Heavenly Father trusts me. I can move on, trusting that He will let me know if I have gone down the wrong road.

A lack of answer when we have a decision to make can also be a signal that the choice ultimately doesn't matter to Him or that it will turn out not to make a difference either way. Elder Dallin H. Oaks shared an experience when he and his wife had to make a decision about something. They prayed and prayed, and no answer came. "We could not imagine why the Lord had not aided us with a confirming or restraining impression," he said. "But it was not long before we learned we did not have to make a decision on that question because something else happened that made a decision unnecessary. The Lord would not guide us in a decision that made no difference."[108]

We also know that Heavenly Father has instructed us through revelation to readily go about our life, prayerfully making choices in the best way that we know how. He does not want us to depend on Him for every decision because He has given us instruction, He has created us with intelligence, He has given us agency, and He trusts us to act. He has revealed to us this counsel: "It is not meet [good, proper] that I should command in all things. . . . Verily I say, men should be anxiously engaged in a good cause, and *do many things of their own free will*, and bring to pass much righteousness; for *the power is in them*, wherein they are agents unto themselves. And inasmuch as men do good they shall in nowise lose their reward" (D&C 58:26–28; italics added). What a comforting promise to know that if we are making choices as best as we know how, then we will be blessed.

Heidi Poelman

When the Answer Is "No"

Sometimes the heavens feel painfully silent because, simply put, the answer to our prayer is no. God has promised us that when the answer to our prayer is yes, we will feel some kind of confirmation that our decision is right. But He also said, "If it be not right you shall have no such feelings" (D&C 9:9).

Kerry shared with me her experience when she finally realized that what she had been praying for was actually not right for her family. This decision had to do with staying in her first marriage, when she and her spouse had three young boys. The marriage was strained and seemed to be having a negative impact on everyone. The choice seemed obvious though—you don't split up a family. They lived in California, where she had no other family, and if she left, she would have no support there. Yet, as she explained, when she prayed to find a way to stay together, "I felt a lot of confusion and darkness, and I felt lost." She finally asked herself if the feelings could mean that Heavenly Father's answer was, "No. You are not supposed to stay." As Kerry explained, "I remember the bed where I knelt and asked, 'Could it be that I am supposed to leave?'" She says that as she prayed about that course of action, of starting a new life with her boys, "I felt light and energy leading me. It was the right thing for me to do, and the right thing for them. It was an opportunity for us to move forward." The decision allowed Kerry to move on to a new path and allowed her boys to maintain a strong relationship with their father while he moved on as well.

That confidence brought by knowing she had followed the Spirit helped her to be strong through all the emotional trials that would follow in making her decision to leave her marriage. Having that witness also helped her boys trust in the decision. As she explained,

> I needed them to have a witness from Heavenly Father. I told them, "Heavenly Father loves us. This is the answer I'm getting for all of us. It's the right choice. I know it is." The Spirit had witnessed to me. That was huge for us to be positive and move forward. We've

ended up being an awesome family. There is a peace in knowing you've done all you can do. I knew I listened and did my best.

Sometimes the hardest silence is the silence when Heavenly Father is directing us with a no. At first, Kerry could not have imagined that what Heavenly Father wanted her to do was leave so she could start a new family. But as she accepted His answer and moved forward following the Spirit, she was able to create a beautiful new life and found the man she was supposed to grow old with. This was a man who could be a wonderful eternal companion as well as a great additional father for her boys. "I see how much I've been blessed," she said. "There is a power in following promptings."

The Savior once taught, "Whatsoever ye ask the Father in my name it shall be given unto you, *that is expedient for you*" (D&C 88:64; italics added). When we are praying for a desired result, Heavenly Father does hear us. He always does. But if it seems like He is not answering, if we are not feeling a confirmation or receiving the answer we want, that request may simply not be right for us. We can trust in knowing that He will ultimately confirm our choices once we decide on the course of action that is right for our eternal happiness. He loves us too much to let us do anything else.

Be Believing

We can trust in our Heavenly Father's unending love and remind ourselves that every answer He grants—whether it is the answer we want or not, given when we want it or not—is actually the answer that is best for our eternal happiness and progression. As Elder Richard G. Scott once said, "Your life will be easier when you accept that what God does in your life is for your *eternal* good."[109] We can know that if we continue to have faith and diligently act in accordance with everything we know about the everlasting gospel, then we will find joy. Maybe not right in this moment, because maybe we need to experience some trials and growth first. But ultimately we will receive answers to our prayers

Heidi Poelman

if we follow the counsel to "pray always, and be believing, and all things shall work together for your good" (D&C 90:24).

President Monson recently shared a poem in general conference that seems to sum up his feelings about prayer and what we can do when we go through those inevitable periods when it seems that God is not listening:

> I know not by what methods rare,
> But this I know, God answers prayer.
> I know that He has given His Word,
> Which tells me prayer is always heard,
> And will be answered, soon or late.
> And so I pray and calmly wait.
> I know not if the blessing sought
> Will come in just the way I thought;
> But leave my prayers with Him alone,
> Whose will is wiser than my own,
> Assured that He will grant my quest,
> Or send some answer far more blest.[110]

Indeed, God answers prayer. It may not be in the way we want or at the time we want, but we can trust that He will do whatever He can to most greatly bless our lives. What He requires from us is a little patience, perspective, and trust. He will come through for His children.

Chapter 12

Lead Me, Guide Me

Teaching Our Children to Hear

THIS BOOK has so far primarily been about the gift that Heavenly Father gives to mothers as we seek to follow His counsel and bless the lives of our children. That gift is the Holy Spirit, which we can utilize for guidance, warnings, and comfort. This chapter explores how we as mothers can give our children a gift as well. When we have embraced the ability to seek after and rely on the Spirit in our lives, we can teach them to do the same. As children see our example, hear us talk about the Spirit, and learn to feel the Spirit in their own lives, they will be immeasurably blessed when they go out into the world to build their own lives. Knowing that our children have that most precious source to rely on, in turn, can give us the confidence that we have done all we can to provide not only for their physical well-being but, more important, for their spiritual well-being as well. If we have done our best to teach them, they will be prepared to make good choices and succeed with happiness in this life and eternal joy in the life to come. What more can we hope for as mothers?

Heidi Poelman

Leading by Example

I love the words in the song "I Am a Child of God" that say, "Lead me, guide me, walk beside me, help me find the way." My mother-in-law, Kerry, once pointed out to me how so much of parenting comes down to that simple phrase. We can spend all the time in the world trying to tell our children how to be, but those words will never be as powerful as when we *show* them how to be with our example. The words *lead, guide,* and *walk beside* don't epitomize a parent sitting in the corner, laying out instructions and pointing a finger of which way to go for ultimate happiness. Rather, they convey the notion of a parent intimately involved in the journey, showing a child just how to do "all that [we] must do to live with him someday."[111]

I remember once thinking how cute it was that my three-year-old daughter often responded to my questions with the phrase "Um . . . sure!" Not just "Sure," but "Um . . . sure." I wondered where she got that, until one day one of my kids asked me a question and I responded with, "Um . . . sure!" Right after I said it, I laughed, realizing that I had been the source of the phrase. That happens a lot, reminding me to be on my guard, demonstrating the behaviors I hope my children will choose to emulate. Whether we are conscious of it or not, our children are watching us and learning from the choices we make and the things we do. This gives us a golden opportunity to teach our children how to listen for and follow the Spirit by what we are doing every day. If we want our children to follow the Spirit, they need to see us do it too.

My neighbor Janis shared with me how her example of prayer once made an impact on her seven-year-old son. It was late in the day, and they needed to make a trip to the grocery store. Upon returning to their car, Janis realized that her keys were missing. "We decided to say a prayer," she said. "Immediately, I found the keys, which had fallen under the seat. Jared was small, but he mentioned that experience in a talk later. It really had an impact on him." What I love about this experience is that, had they just kept looking, they probably would have eventually found the keys. But this mother took an opportunity to show her son, by her example, what to do when you need help: you pray.

Another mother, Carla, shared her experience of praying one night when her teenage son was out past his curfew. She had been worried about him, and so she got down on her knees to ask for God's help bringing him home. She found out later that her son and his friends, just old enough to drive, had gotten into a run-in with some kids from another school who were taunting them and pursuing them on the road. Carla's son described it as the scariest night of his life. When he finally got home, he found his mother on her knees. He said, "That's why we're here. You prayed us home." I imagine that moment had a life-altering impact on this young man's testimony of prayer.

Children can even watch how we seek to be worthy of the Spirit when we show them the process of repentance. Kerry is a big believer that because her children watched her go through the process of trial, error, repentance, and renewal, they learned about that incredible process too. They learned that, rather than feeling like you can't come back from a mistake, repentance is a beautiful, ongoing process that we can embrace as we pursue our quest to become like God.

"I had to be willing to humble myself and correct mistakes," she said. "The cool part is that while I was figuring it out, I was open to my children watching. I would make a mistake and say, 'You know what? I handled that wrong. But I've repented, and I want to start again.'" Kerry's children were able to see her make mistakes but then also see up close how repentance works. I love her approach. As Scott and I have tried to figure out the best way to raise our own kids, we try to follow her example and always be open to apologizing and showing them that making a mistake is okay as long as you make it right. Then we can have the Spirit with us again.

Every time we pray, every time we talk about feeling the Spirit in our lives, and every time we show our children that we are seeking to be worthy, we teach them how to do all of those things too. That is our duty as parents. As Elder Robert D. Hales said, "For all of us, doing our duty to God as parents and leaders *begins* with leading by example—consistently and diligently living gospel principles at home. This takes daily determination and diligence."[112] If we can show our children in little ways every day how we feel about praying to our Father in Heaven and seeking the Spirit in our lives, then they will begin to build their own testimonies of how the Spirit can bless their lives as well.

Talking about the Spirit

One important way to teach our children about the Spirit is to talk about it with them regularly. My neighbor Laura is a tremendous example of how to do this. As she said, "We tried to take every opportunity to share when we felt it and tried to help them understand what a prompting felt like. As a parent, you're so focused on helping them learn the things that are going to give them the help they need to navigate this earthly life. They are discovering so many new things in their youth. I took every opportunity I could to make it a teaching or understanding moment."

One way Laura and her husband took those opportunities was to pray with their children when they had decisions to make while they were growing up. Then a day or two later, they would ask their children about their feelings and about what the Spirit was prompting them to do. I remember doing this with my daughter Ellie when she was trying to decide what instrument she wanted to learn. It was down to piano, violin, or cello. After we listened to lots of different music and made a chart with all the upsides and downsides of each instrument, we asked Ellie to pray about it. Then we talked with her about her feelings and helped guide her through her decision. That experience was just one way Ellie is learning how to make a decision with the Spirit.

Kerry made this an important goal while she was raising her children. She said, "When I'd be talking with a child, I'd ask them, 'What feels like the right thing to do? What rings true to you? What feels like the right thing for you right now?' They would learn to explore. They were able to recognize the Spirit and feel empowered to make decisions." What a blessing for these children to grow up with parents who coached them in how to make decisions guided by the Spirit! This is something I hope for my own children. I figure if they can learn that skill when they are young, making relatively small decisions, then they will also be prepared after years of practice to make all the tough decisions that come later, whether it's choosing to go on a mission, what college to attend, what career field to study, or whom to marry. The decisions that impact these little ones' lives will come again and again. They just need the tools to choose wisely.

Talking about how the Spirit has guided our own decisions as parents is another powerful teaching opportunity. My friend Shannon expressed to me how she and her husband have tried to do this: "We've always loved to just talk about great experiences from our lives, like decisions to go on a mission or get married, or how the process of Adam and Lucy's adoptions were so clearly led by the Spirit," she said. "We don't reserve those just for designated teaching moments when it seems scripted. Instead we make it part of normal, everyday talk: around the dinner table, in the car, whenever something reminds us of it. We'll make it fun, funny, awesome, energetic, and, most of all, real!"

Similarly, my friend Julie shared with me how much her children love hearing about real experiences with the Spirit. "I find that we teach our children to seek the Spirit by bringing it up frequently throughout the day," she said. "They love hearing stories about our lives and the lives of our ancestors and how we have listened to the still, small voice." I love the reminder that came from these great women—talking about the Spirt makes an impact. Every chance we have, we can talk with our children about experiences with the Spirit in our lives. The more we talk about our experiences, the more real and normal it will become for our children to seek and feel the Spirit too.

Heidi Poelman

Pointing Out the Presence of the Spirit

Pointing out when the Spirit is near is another way to help our children learn what it feels like. My neighbor Laura was able to discuss the promptings of the Spirit with her son Carter one day when they were on their way home from school, a story I mentioned previously. Laura listened to a prompting in the car that caused her to stop before she would have been T-boned by a woman on her cell phone who sped through a red light. As Laura said, "I explained to Carter that I was guided by the Spirit to stop. I talked with him about following promptings when you get them. They can sometimes save your life." Laura and Carter expressed their thanks for the spiritual prompting in their prayers that night.

What a marvelous opportunity to teach her son about the life-altering power of the Spirit. She could have easily let that moment pass by with a sigh of relief, inwardly thanking her Father in Heaven for the warning. Instead, she taught her son something powerful that day about listening to the promptings that might alter life forever.

Sometimes the Spirit is present in our home or wherever we are, and though our children may feel something, they don't recognize it as the Spirit until we point it out. Scott and I try to be aware of those teaching moments when we have just talked about something or watched or listened to something that has brought the Spirit. We'll ask our kids, "Do you feel that? What do you feel?" Once when we asked our little three-year-old daughter Addie that question, she said, "My heart is shining!" I love that description. We smiled and explained to her just what was causing that feeling in her heart. Regularly pointing out when the Holy Ghost is near helps our children, little by little, learn how the Spirit feels and functions so they can begin to recognize it in their lives.

We can also help our children understand the comforting power of the Spirit when they are experiencing pain or sorrow. My friend Cary shared with me a story of how her six-year-old daughter, Hannah, learned about the Spirit one night when she was missing her "Grandpa Great," who had passed away. Hannah had been close to this relative and thought about him often. One night when Hannah was missing Grandpa Great, Cary took the time to explain where he was and suggested that Hannah pray for comfort to know he was okay. Hannah went back to her room, and then half an hour later, she came back to her mother with tears in her eyes.

"She told me and my husband about how she had said a prayer telling her Heavenly Father how she missed her Grandpa Great and how she hoped he was okay," Cary said. "She said she felt a feeling come into her heart that made her cry. She said she knew Grandpa Great was in a good place and that she would see him again." The experience was a memorable one for Cary, as she recognized the power in these teaching moments. As she said, "I was touched by this experience and was reminded of the importance of teaching our children to turn to the Spirit for comfort and answers."

Cary's story is a beautiful reminder to me that, in addition to a listening ear and plenty of hugs and kisses, we can offer our children the knowledge that the Holy Ghost is always near when they are in need of comfort. Then when they do feel that reassuring peace inside, we can help them recognize what they are feeling.

Creating the Right Environment

If we want our children to have experiences with the Spirit, we need to create the kind of environment where the Spirit can dwell. That includes everything that impacts the atmosphere of our home, such as the music we play, whether the television is on all the time, the level of chaos and noise in our home, the way family members interact with each other, and even the artwork on our walls.

The home where Scott grew up is a glowing example of an environment that is conducive to the Spirit. I noticed it right away when I first started dating Scott—people were kind and respectful to each other, the home was clean and organized, the family prioritized listening to and playing beautiful music, and inspiring pictures and quotes covered the walls. Of course, no family is perfect. My first observations were probably slightly skewed from reality, considering that having company puts people on their best behavior and tips the scales of cleanliness up a notch. Still, I knew it was a priority for Kerry to create a warm and comfortable environment where children could feel inspired, and I have continued to observe the same environment every time I go to their home. Here's how she describes the importance she places on creating that sacred space:

> We still had fun things, like video games and movies, but nothing that was offensive to the Spirit. Pictures of temples and Christ hang in every room. I wanted to show it, wear it, be it. Why would we want to hide what we believe in? We can buy more into what the world says is beautiful, or we can create a space where our children can feel the Spirit. It's just how it is. They may not even notice it until they are twenty-eight and come back home. I'm not going to cater to the world.

The point here is not to make moms feel overwhelmed with the prospect of keeping a spotless, quiet home when kids, by nature, create mess and chaos (at least in my experience). The Spirit doesn't need perfection. It doesn't need silence. The Spirit can dwell in a home where members of a family are trying their best to live gospel principles, to be their best selves, and to play with, love, and find joy in each other, even while making mistakes along the way. We won't be perfect, but we can strive every day to create an environment where the Spirit can be.

That environment can even extend beyond our home to anywhere we happen to be. Indeed, we can create a space that allows the Spirit to be with us wherever we go, whether that's at church, school, work, a dance recital, a football game, or even a hospital. When I was interviewing Kerry for this project, she reminded me of when Ellie split her head open during a sleepover at Gram and Papa's (Kerry and Mark's) house. Ellie tripped on some bedding when the kids were playing tag and hit her head on the corner of a bed, splitting the skin open above her eye. We knew she needed stitches, so Kerry, Scott, Ellie, and I got in the car and drove to the hospital.

While Ellie was lying on the bed in the ER, in pain and afraid, I had the idea to sing to her. I didn't think much of it other than that I wanted to comfort my little girl. This is what Kerry saw: "I remember you were singing Primary songs to her up at her ear, to help her concentrate on the Spirit. How sweet and perfect it was to have a mom singing songs. It didn't matter who walked by. You were focused on bringing a spirit of peace for her and bringing her comfort."

Again, I hadn't really thought about creating an environment where the Spirit could bring comfort, but that's exactly what happened. Ellie calmed down, listened to the words, and seemed to find a place of peace and courage. That wasn't just me—that was the Spirit. We can open the door for the Spirit to dwell no matter where we are. If we create a space around us where our children can feel peace, love, strength, respect, and happiness, then we are giving them their best chance to have experiences with the Spirit.

Be Not Afraid

Part of teaching our children to follow the Spirit's counsel is to be confident when we feel spiritual guidance, even when it goes against what our children want. In those moments, we must choose to "be strong and of a good courage" and "be not afraid" (Joshua 1:9) to make tough choices.

Elder Larry R. Lawrence of the Quorum of the Seventy shared a story about when the Spirit was guiding him and his wife to an answer that they knew would be disappointing to their son. Their seventeen-year-old son wanted to go on a weekend trip with some friends, all of whom Elder Lawrence describes as good kids. Their son asked permission to go, and Elder Lawrence wanted to say yes. Yet for some reason, he felt uncomfortable about the trip and felt like the Spirit was guiding him to say no. He shared his feelings with his wife, who felt like they needed to listen to that voice. When they told their son they didn't want him to go on the trip, he was disappointed and asked why. Elder Lawrence said that he didn't know why. "I just don't feel good about it," he explained, "and I love you too much to ignore these feelings inside." He was surprised by his son's response, which was, "That's OK, Dad. I understand."[113]

What an impressive young man to have such faith in his parents! But also, what impressive parents to have such faith in their Father in Heaven, whom they knew was guiding them along (though they didn't know why). Parents, by nature, want to help their children be happy. We want to say yes when we can. But these parents knew that their son's long-term well-being was more important than his temporary happiness, and they had the courage to follow the Spirit. That's not easy. But think of what our children see when they watch us make a tough choice in order to follow a prompting.

Elder Lawrence encouraged parents to be united in making those tough decisions and to always follow the promptings of the Spirit. He said, "If either parent doesn't feel good about something, then permission should not be granted. If either feels uncomfortable about a movie, a television show, a video game, a party, a dress, a swimsuit, or an Internet activity, have the courage to support each other. . . . When you take the easy way out by saying and doing nothing, you may be enabling destructive behavior."[114] By having the courage to follow the Spirit, even with tough parenting choices, we show our children how important God's guidance is to us and how much we love them. If they are not grateful in the moment, then hopefully they will understand in the long run.

The Blessing of Confidence

As much as we want to give our children everything, we cannot hand them a testimony of the gospel, and we cannot give them the Spirit. They must do their part while we do ours. What we can do is lead them, guide them, and walk beside them on their journey as they learn how to seek after, identify, and be worthy of the

Spirit in their lives. Elder Robert D. Hales said, "We can teach them to walk in the light, but that light cannot be borrowed. They must earn it for themselves. . . . They must understand who they are and who Heavenly Father wants them to become."[115] It is our job to lead them and guide them while they are young. Then they will choose what to do with what they have been given. The more we can teach them to rely on the Spirit, the greater confidence we can have as they go on their mortal journey.

Once we have played our part to teach them who they are and how to navigate this life with the Spirit, they can be well on their way to living a good and joyful life. Our children may even surprise us when they demonstrate the spiritual skills we've worked so hard to teach them. My neighbor Laura's son Colton showed his testimony of utilizing the Spirit when it came time to decide which college to attend. Colton had received scholarships to Arizona State University and the University of Utah. He decided that if he could get a scholarship to the Honors College at ASU, then he would go there. He got everything he wanted from both schools, so he decided to pray about his decision to go to ASU. Laura thought the decision was made.

"A couple of days later, he informed us that he had received a strong impression that Utah is where he should go to school," Laura said. "We were a little surprised until he opened his mission call to the Arizona Tempe Mission, right where ASU is located! He worked teaching the gospel to the kids on campus for many months." Not only was Colton able to serve his mission in a place where he *didn't* attend college, but he also met a girl at the University of Utah who is now his wife. Colton didn't know what was on the road ahead of him when he started praying about his decision, but Heavenly Father did. And Colton knew enough to follow that voice.

Laura and her husband, who had worked for years to teach their son about following the Spirit, actually got to watch him do exactly what they had taught him to do: study, ponder, pray, and follow the Spirit. Then they all got to see *why* Heavenly Father had prompted him in that particular path. As a mother of young kids, I can only imagine the joy of knowing that my grown children have the tools to go about their lives and follow Heavenly Father's guidance as they make their choices. What greater gift could we possibly give our children?

We live in a beautiful and wonderful world, which also happens to be rife with contention, challenge, and temptation. I love how my friend Cary describes her hope for her children as they grow up in this world:

> I believe that teaching our children to rely on the Spirit is the one way we can empower them to be successful. My hope and prayer is that as my children get older and spend more time in situations where I am not present, they will be strong and rely on the Spirit to help them distinguish between truth and error. Relying on the Spirit will help give my children strength to stand tall when it would be easier to go with the crowd, will give them courage to do hard things, and will give them peace when they do so.

Teaching our children to follow and utilize the Spirit has the potential to affect their whole lives as they make choices, deal with trials, and build their testimonies of their Savior. Think of everything you hope for your children. What choices do you want them to make? What path do you want them to follow? Who do you hope they will become? As my friend Melissa described,

> I want them to be good people, to desire to make correct choices, to resist temptations, to be able to be leaders and examples, to know how to ask for help, to know how to seek peace and comfort in trying times, to know how to receive answers to prayers, to go on missions, and to get married in the temple. I don't think it would be as easy, or in some cases even possible, for them to do those things if they can't or don't feel and recognize the Spirit.

Every effort we make through our example, our attitude, and our conversations, and in the environment we strive to create, has the potential to teach our children about the Spirit. If we can give them that gift to seek and know the Spirit when they are young, then we can be confident that when we send them out into the world, away from the shelter of their parents' roof, they will have everything they need to build a righteous and happy life.

Speaking to a group of religious educators, Elder Richard G. Scott once said, "Those you teach live in a world subject to challenges and temptations. I am convinced that without the help of the Spirit an individual will have difficulty avoiding transgression in the world of today. . . . If you accomplish nothing else in your relationship with your students than to help them recognize and follow the promptings of the Spirit, you will bless their lives immeasurably and eternally."[116] If that applies to teachers, how much more does it apply to parents? We have the power to bless our children's lives *immeasurably and eternally* if we can teach them how to follow the Spirit every day of their lives.

Chapter 13

The Promise

THIS BOOK is the result of one mother's journey to learn more about helping her children succeed in life. *Succeed* is an interesting word. I don't mean worldly success. This wasn't a quest to learn how to give my children the most respectable careers, how to make loads of money, or how to live so they can receive the accolades and honors of men. I wanted to know how to help my children reach their potential to follow their Savior, to discover the amazing beauties of the earth, to enjoy learning and study, to experience the wonder of building families of their own, to contribute to making the world a better place through service, and ultimately to feel the *joy* of a life well lived. That's a tall order, yes. But I believe it is possible if we can teach our children to utilize this one most important gift—the Holy Spirit—every day of their lives.

Heavenly Father's gift to us as mothers is the ability to communicate with Him while we raise our children—to see a glimpse of what He sees, to feel a drop of the love He feels, and to know a bit about what He knows is possible for each one of us. That is all available to us through His Spirit. After searching the scriptures, studying words of the prophets, interviewing incredible mothers, thinking over my own experiences, and praying to know more, here is what I have learned:

Heidi Poelman

- Heavenly Father's work and glory has everything to do with the success of His children here on earth (see Moses 1:39). He wants us to find joy and to make it home.
- Heavenly Father has great trust in mothers, the women He asks to shepherd along His precious spirit children. As we are given the privilege of bearing, raising, and nurturing these children, and He allows us to be cocreators with Him.
- Heavenly Father communicates with us through a key messenger, the Holy Ghost (or Holy Spirit).
- The Holy Ghost communicates with our spirits in a way unlike the way we receive messages with our physical senses. It typically speaks softly to our mind through our thoughts and to our hearts through our feelings.
- The Spirit is available at any time to direct us, warn us, and comfort us.
- Heavenly Father is occasionally willing to intervene if we need to change course.
- God communicates with us through priesthood blessings. Mothers are in a unique position to understand the needs of their families and to feel promptings for when their children may need a priesthood blessing.
- Angels communicate through the power of the Holy Ghost and are often present to comfort and direct us in our times of need.
- We can strengthen our ability to hear and feel messages from our Father when we are worthy, have faith, pray diligently, listen carefully, attend the temple, take opportunities to fast, and create an environment where the Spirit can dwell.
- Occasionally, Heavenly Father waits to answer our prayers, whether that is because the timing is not yet right, the answer is no, or the wait is for our own good while we develop faith and patience. We can trust that He will eventually answer our prayers in whatever way is best for us.

- If we choose to seek after and listen for the Spirit in our lives every day as we are raising our children, we will be blessed, strengthened, and directed for good.
- We can teach our children to utilize the Spirit in their lives, which can help guide them as they make all the decisions that will come their way, warn them when they are in trouble, and comfort them in times of need. That knowledge, in turn, gives us as mothers the confidence that our children have the most important tool they need to find success and joy throughout their lives.

When I wrapped up my interview with Kerry, the woman who inspired this book, she testified to me of how important the Spirit has been to her as she raised her five children. While she looked back on her time doing her best to raise these five souls with her spouse, these were the thoughts and feelings that came to mind:

> Heavenly Father and the Holy Ghost have been active in our family. I'm in the season of joy now for having invested so much. It's not just joy in how many degrees they've earned, but the true joy that comes in knowing I did my best, and I asked the Spirit to guide me. That journey has led to joy in my relationships. My children are my best friends. I asked them actively to work alongside me and make good choices. Not everyone makes those choices. I feel grateful to my children for choosing as they have and pray that they keep following the Spirit throughout their lives.

Kerry is now feeling the fruits of her labors of love. Of course, trying our best to listen for and act on the promptings of the Spirit is no guarantee. Wrapped up in all of this is the understanding that our children have their agency and will make their own choices in life—some that will make us proud, some that will make us smile, and some that will break our hearts. We have to accept that agency is part of the plan. The promise is not an if-then statement for creating perfect children. Rather, the promise is about what we gain if we are willing to seek our Eternal Father's counsel.

Heidi Poelman

The scriptures spell it out plainly: *"Draw near* unto me and I will draw near unto you; *seek me* diligently and ye shall find me; *ask,* and ye shall receive; *knock,* and it shall be opened unto you" (D&C 88:63; italics added). That is the promise: if we allow Him into our lives, He will be there. We won't be perfect, and neither will our children. But if we can look back and say that we sought our Heavenly Father's guidance, we tried our best to live according to His counsel, we accepted His comfort, and we taught our children how to do the same, then we can know we gave it our all. The rest will be up to them.

It won't be easy. Nothing that's really worth it ever is. The reward goes beyond momentary happiness. It is the culmination of struggle and effort, sacrifice and love. It is *earned.* Our Father in Heaven wants each of His children to have that joy of a life well lived. He wants us to receive everything He has to offer. What He asks of us is simply to do our part: to draw close to Him, to seek Him, to ask for Him, to knock at the door where He is waiting, and to partner with Him while we raise our children.

I love what Elder Richard G. Scott had to say about what can happen should we choose to utilize this most precious gift—the ability to communicate with our Father in Heaven. He said, "You will be inspired and can have power beyond your own capacity. You can qualify through that divine power to be instruments in the hands of God to accomplish what you could not do alone."[117] Indeed, we *can* have power to do what we could not do alone. We can have God on our side, to lift, direct, comfort, and strengthen us every day of our lives. As a mother, that is a gift I plan to cherish.

Notes, Impressions, and Promptings

Heidi Poelman

_____

_____

_____

_____

_____

_____

_____

_____

_____

_____

_____

_____

_____

_____

_____

_____

_____

_____

_____

Heidi Poelman

_____

_____

_____

_____

_____

_____

_____

_____

_____

_____

_____

_____

_____

_____

_____

_____

_____

_____

Heidi Poelman

Heidi Poelman

_____

_____

_____

_____

_____

_____

_____

_____

_____

_____

_____

_____

_____

_____

_____

_____

_____

_____

Heidi Poelman

_____
_____
_____
_____
_____
_____
_____
_____
_____
_____
_____
_____
_____
_____
_____
_____
_____

Heidi Poelman

_____

_____

_____

_____

_____

_____

_____

_____

_____

_____

_____

_____

_____

_____

_____

_____

_____

_____

_____

_____

_____

_____

_____

_____

_____

_____

_____

_____

_____

_____

_____

_____

_____

_____

_____

_____

_____

Heidi Poelman

_____

_____

_____

_____

_____

_____

_____

_____

_____

_____

_____

_____

_____

_____

_____

_____

Endnotes

1. Beck, "'And upon the Handmaids.'"
2. Faust, "Lifeline of Prayer."
3. "The Family," 102.
4. "O My Father."
5. Dew, *Women and the Priesthood*.
6. Hinckley, Third Stake conference.
7. Cowley, *Matthew Cowley Speaks*.
8. McKay, *Gospel Ideals*.
9. Holland, "Motherhood."
10. Dew, *Women and the Priesthood*.
11. Hales, "Our Duty to God."
12. McKay, *Gospel Ideals*.
13. *Random House Dictionary*; Wilson, *Old Testament Word Studies*.
14. Snow, Conference Report.
15. Talmage, *Articles of Faith*, 286.
16. Lund, *Voice of the Lord*, 78–79.
17. Ibid., 12.
18. Bednar, "Receive the Holy Ghost."
19. Ibid.
20. Lund, *Voice of the Lord*, 21.
21. Ibid., 48.
22. Durham, *Wilford Woodruff*, 45.
23. Packer, "Candle of the Lord," 53.
24. Eyring, "Life Founded in Light and Truth."

25. Scott, "Supernal Gift of Prayer."

26. Lund, *Voice of the Lord*, 54.

27. Kimball, *Spencer W. Kimball*, 258.

28. Oaks, "Teaching and Learning."

29. Lund, *Voice of the Lord*, 54.

30. Ibid., 57.

31. Kimball, *Faith Precedes the Miracle*, 65–66; italics added.

32. Lund, *Voice of the Lord*, 165.

33. *Wilford Woodruff*, 296.

34. Smith, *Prophet Joseph Smith*, 98.

35. Hinckley, *Gordon B. Hinckley*, 261.

36. Lund, *Voice of the Lord*, 201.

37. McConkie, "Agency or Inspiration."

38. Kimball, *Revelation*, 76.

39. Scott, *21 Principles*, 95–96.

40. Ibid., 23.

41. Lund, *Voice of the Lord*, 74.

42. Smith, *Joseph Smith*, 151.

43. Benson, *Ezra Taft Benson*, 114.

44. Oaks, "Teaching and Learning."

45. Packer, "Washed Clean."

46. Lund, *Voice of the Lord*, 114.

47. Scott, *21 Principles*, 44.

48. Lund, *Voice of the Lord*, 115.

49. Scott, "Supernal Gift of Prayer."

50. Benson, *Come unto Christ*, 20.

51. Smith, *Gospel Doctrine*, 139.

52. Anderson, "Power in the Priesthood."

53. *Nauvoo Relief Society Minute Book*.

54. Dew, *Women and the Priesthood*, 119–20.

55. Ibid., 124.

56. Ibid., 125.

57. See *Merriam-Webster* online dictionary.

58. Lund, *Voice of the Lord*, 35–36.

59. Holland, "Ministry of Angels"; italics added.

60. *Daughters in My Kingdom*, 169.
61. Faust, "Refiner's Fire."
62. Talmage, *Articles of Faith*, 96–97.
63. Bednar, "Receive the Holy Ghost."
64. Packer, "Personal Revelation."
65. Faust, "Great Imitator."
66. Packer, "Personal Revelation."
67. *George Albert Smith*, 117.
68. Scott, "Recognize Answers to Prayers."
69. Lund, *Voice of the Lord*, 146.
70. Packer, "Personal Revelation."
71. Scott, "Supernal Gift of Prayer."
72. Ibid.
73. *Spencer W. Kimball*, 146–47.
74. Scott, "Supernal Gift of Prayer."
75. Hales, "Holy Scriptures."
76. McConkie, *Doctrines of the Restoration*, 243.
77. Lee, *Stand Ye in Holy Places*, 159.
78. Packer, "Reverence Invites Revelation."
79. Eyring, "As a Child."
80. *Harold B. Lee*, 54; also see Isaiah 58:6–9.
81. Scott, "To Acquire Spiritual Guidance."
82. Ibid.
83. Scott, "Helping Others Be Spiritually Led," 57.
84. Benson, *Ezra Taft Benson*, 251.
85. Benson, "Book of Mormon."
86. Oaks, *The Lord's Way*, 37–38.
87. Packer, "Candle of the Lord."
88. Nelson, "Spiritual Capacity."
89. Lund, *Voice of the Lord*, 146–47.
90. Packer, "Prayers and Answers."
91. Hinckley, *Gordon B. Hinckley*, 469.
92. Scott, "Supernal Gift of Prayer."
93. Packer, "Prayers and Answers."
94. Hunter, *Howard W. Hunter*, 39.

Endnotes

95. Lund, *Voice of the Lord*, 176.

96. ten Boom, *Hiding Place*, 12.

97. Burton, "Turning Our Hearts."

98. Scott, "Supernal Gift of Prayer."

99. Oaks, *The Lord's Way*, 36.

100. Scott, "To Acquire Spiritual Guidance."

101. Uchtdorf, "Living the Gospel Joyful."

102. Oaks, "In His Own Time," 22, 24.

103. Poelman, *Simeon Solution*.

104. Hagman, "Heavenly Father Said No."

105. Scott, *21 Principles*, 33–34.

106. Scott, "Supernal Gift of Prayer."

107. Ibid.

108. Oaks, *The Lord's Way*, 37.

109. Scott, "Supernal Gift of Prayer."

110. Hickok, "Prayer"; quoted in Thomas S. Monson, "We Never Walk Alone," *Ensign*, November 2013.

111. "I Am a Child of God."

112. Hales, "Our Duty to God"; italics added.

113. Lawrence, "Courageous Parenting."

114. Ibid.

115. Hales, "Our Duty to God."

116. Scott, "Helping Others Be Spiritually Led."

117. Scott, *21 Principles*, 17.

Sources

Anderson, Neil L. "Power in the Priesthood." *Ensign*, November 2013.

Beck, Julie B. "'And upon the Handmaids in Those Days Will I Pour Out My Spirit.'" *Ensign*, May 2010.

Bednar, David A. "Receive the Holy Ghost." *Ensign*, November 2010.

Benson, Ezra Taft. *The Teachings of Ezra Taft Benson*. Salt Lake City: Bookcraft, 1988.

Benson, Ezra Taft. *Come Unto Christ*. Salt Lake City: Deseret Book, 1983.

Benson, Ezra Taft. "The Book of Mormon and the Doctrine and Covenants." *Ensign*, May 1987.

Burton, Linda K. "Turning Our Hearts to the Voice of the Spirit." CES Devotional for Young Adults, Brigham Young University–Idaho, March 2, 2014.

Cowley, Matthew. *Matthew Cowley Speaks*. Salt Lake City: Deseret Book, 1954, 109.

Daughters in My Kingdom. Salt Lake City: The Church of Jesus Christ of Latter-day Saints, 2011.

Dew, Sheri. *Women and the Priesthood: What One Mormon Woman Believes*. Salt Lake City: Deseret Book, 2013.

Durham, G. Homer, comp. *The Discourses of Wilford Woodruff*. Salt Lake City: Bookcraft, 1946.

Eyring, Henry B. "A Life Founded in Light and Truth." BYU Devotional, August 15, 2000.

Sources

Eyring, Henry B. "As a Child." *Ensign*, May 2006.

Faust, James E. "The Lifeline of Prayer." *Ensign*, May 2002.

Faust, James E. "'The Great Imitator.'" *Ensign*, November 1987, 33.

Faust, James E. "The Refiner's Fire." *Ensign*, May 1979, 53.

Hagman, Angelica. "Heavenly Father Said No—and Yes." *Ensign*, August 2014.

Hales, Robert D. "Our Duty to God: The Mission of Parents and Leaders to the Rising Generation." *Ensign*, May 2010.

Hales, Robert D. "Holy Scriptures: The Power of God unto Our Salvation." *Ensign*, November 2006, 26–27.

Hickok, Eliza M. "Prayer." In *The Best-Loved Religious Poems*. Compiled by James G. Lawson. Grand Rapids: Fleming H. Revell, 1933, 160.

Hinckley, Gordon B. *Teachings of Gordon B. Hinckley*. Salt Lake City: Deseret Book, 1997.

Hinckley, Gordon B. Salt Lake University Third Stake conference, 3 November 1996; in *Church News*, 1 March 1997, 2.

Holland, Jeffrey R. "Motherhood: An Eternal Partnership with God." LDS.org, https://www.lds.org/pages/motherhood?lang=eng.

Holland, Jeffrey R. "The Ministry of Angels." *Ensign*, November 2008.

Hunter, Howard W. *The Teachings of Howard W. Hunter*. Salt Lake City: Deseret Book, 1997.

"I Am a Child of God." *Hymns*, no. 301.

Kimball, Spencer W. *Faith Precedes the Miracle*. Salt Lake City: Deseret Book, 1972.

Kimball, Spencer W. "Revelation: The Word of the Lord to His Prophets." *Ensign*, May 1977.

Kimball, Spencer W. *The Teachings of Spencer W. Kimball*. Edited by Edward L. Kimball. Salt Lake City: Bookcraft, 1982.

Lawrence, Larry R. "Courageous Parenting." *Ensign*, November 2010.

Lee, Harold B. *Stand Ye in Holy Places*. Salt Lake City: Deseret Book, 1974.

Lund, Gerald N. *Hearing the Voice of the Lord: Principles and Patterns of Personal Revelation*. Salt Lake City: Deseret Book, 2007.

McConkie, Bruce R. "Agency or Inspiration—Which?" BYU Devotional, February 27, 1973.

McConkie, Bruce R. *Doctrines of the Restoration: Sermons and Writing of Bruce R. McConkie*. Edited and arranged by Mark L. McConkie. Salt Lake City: Bookcraft, 1989.

McKay, David O. *Gospel Ideals*. Salt Lake City: Improvement Era, 1953, 453–54.

Merriam-Webster online dictionary. "Receive" http://www.merriam-webster.com/dictionary/receive.

Nelson, M. Russell. "Spiritual Capacity." *Ensign*, November 1997.

Nauvoo Relief Society Minute Book, 28 April 1842.

"O My Father." *Hymns*, no. 292.

Oaks, Dallin H. *The Lord's Way*. Salt Lake City: Deseret Book, 1991.

Oaks, Dallin H. "Teaching and Learning by the Spirit." *Ensign*, March 1997, 14.

Oaks, Dallin H. "In His Own Time, in His Own Way." *Ensign*, August 2013.

Packer, Boyd K. "Personal Revelation: The Gift, the Test, and the Promise." *Ensign*, November 1994.

Packer, Boyd K. "The Candle of the Lord." *Ensign*, January 1983, 51–56.

Packer, Boyd K. "Prayers and Answers." *Ensign*, November 1979.

Packer, Boyd K. "Reverence Invites Revelation." *Ensign*, November 1991.

Packer, Boyd K. "Washed Clean." *Ensign*, April 1997.

Poelman, Anne Osborn. *The Simeon Solution: One Woman's Spiritual Odyssey*. Salt Lake City: Deseret Book, 2008.

Pratt, Parley P. *Key to the Science of Theology*. Classics in Mormon Literature ed. Salt Lake City: Deseret Book, 1978.

Sources

Richards, Stephen L. In Conference Report, April 1950.

Scott, Richard G. "Helping Others Be Spiritually Led." *Teaching Seminary Preservice Readings Religion 370, 471, and 475*. Salt Lake City: The Church of Jesus Christ of Latter-day Saints, 2004, 55–57.

Scott, Richard G. "Learning to Recognize Answers to Prayers." *Ensign*, November 1989, 30.

Scott, Richard G. "Using the Supernal Gift of Prayer." *Ensign*, May 2007.

Scott, Richard G. *21 Principles: Divine Truths to Help You Live by the Spirit*. Salt Lake City: Deseret Book, 2013.

Scott, Richard G. "To Acquire Spiritual Guidance." *Ensign*, November 2009.

Smith, Joseph. *Teachings of the Prophet Joseph Smith*. Selected by Joseph Fielding Smith. Salt Lake City: Deseret Book, 1976.

Smith, Joseph F. *Gospel Doctrine: Sermons and Writings*. 5th edition. Salt Lake City: Deseret Book, 1939.

Snow, Lorenzo. In Conference Report, April 1899, 52.

Stevenson, Mary. "Footprints in the Sand." http://www.footprints-inthe-sand.com/index.php?page=Poem/Poem.php

Talmage, James E. *The Articles of Faith*. Salt Lake City: Deseret Book, 1924.

Teachings of Presidents of the Church: George Albert Smith. Salt Lake City: The Church of Jesus Christ of Latter-day Saints, 2011, 117.

Teachings of the Presidents of the Church: Harold B. Lee. Salt Lake City: The Church of Jesus Christ of Latter-day Saints, 2000.

Teachings of Presidents of the Church: Spencer W. Kimball. Salt Lake City: The Church of Jesus Christ of Latter-day Saints, 2006.

Teachings of Presidents of the Church: Wilford Woodruff. Salt Lake City: The Church of Jesus Christ of Latter-day Saints, 2011.

ten Boom, Corrie, Elizabeth Sherrill, and John Sherrill. *The Hiding Place*. 35th Anniversary ed. Grand Rapids: Chosen Books, 2006, 12.

"The Family: A Proclamation to the World." *Ensign*, November 1995, 102.

The Random House Dictionary of the English Language. Edited by Jess Stein and Laurence Urdang. New York: Random House, 1966.

Uchtdorf, Dieter F. "Living the Gospel Joyful." *Ensign*, November 2014.

Wilson, William. *Old Testament Word Studies: An English Hebrew and Chaldee Lexicon and Concordance*. 3d ed. Grand Rapids: Kregel Publications, 1978.

About the Author

Heidi Poelman has always loved learning about topics that can strengthen and inspire families. In addition to *A Mother's Greatest Gift*, Heidi is the author of *A Is for Abinadi: An Alphabet Book of Scripture Heroes* and *The Two-Minute Marriage Project: Simple Secrets for Staying in Love*. She received her degrees in communication from Brigham Young University (BA) and Wake Forest University (MA). Heidi and her husband, Scott, live in Utah and are the parents of four children. Learn more at www.heidipoelman.com.